Dancing the Data

LESLEY

Series in Arts & Education

Elijah Mirochnik
General Editor

Vol. 5

PETER LANG
New York • Washington, D.C./Baltimore • Bern
Frankfurt am Main • Berlin • Brussels • Vienna • Oxford

Dancing the Data

EDITED BY

Carl Bagley and Mary Beth Cancienne

PETER LANG
New York • Washington, D.C./Baltimore • Bern
Frankfurt am Main • Berlin • Brussels • Vienna • Oxford

Library of Congress Cataloging-in-Publication Data

Dancing the data / [edited by] Carl Bagley and Mary Beth Cancienne.
p. cm. — (Lesley University series in arts and education; v. 5)
Includes bibliographical references (p.) and index.
1. Communication and the arts—United States. 2. Education—Research—United States. I. Bagley, Carl. II. Cancienne, Mary Beth. III. Series.
NX180.C65 D36 700'.7'2073—dc21 2001038383
0-8204-5525-3
ISSN 1524-0177

Die Deutsche Bibliothek-CIP-Einheitsaufnahme

Dancing the data / ed. by Carl Bagley and Mary Beth Cancienne.
–New York; Washington, D.C./Baltimore; Bern;
Frankfurt am Main; Berlin; Brussels; Vienna; Oxford: Lang.
(Lesley University series in arts and education; Vol. 5)
0-8204-5525-3

dancingdata.com

Cover design by Joni Holst

Contents

PART TWO MUSIC AND POETRY DATA

PART THREE VISUAL ARTS DATA

Acknowledgments[1]

We would like to thank Kent Schwager, owner of the Corner Meal Plan in Charlottesville, Virginia, and founder and CEO of Vmeals.com for supporting this visionary project; Scott Wilson, president of 2flydesigns.com, for the production of the book cover and CD ROM; Terry Jenoure for giving us permission to use her image for the book cover; Elijah Mirochnik for including this project in the Lesley University Series in Arts and Education; the contributors for their dedication to artful scholarship; and our family, friends, colleagues, and research participants for their support.

1. Bagley, C., & Cancienne, M. B. (2001). *Educational research and intertextual forms of (re)presentation: The case for dancing the data*, 7(2), 221–237. Permission to reprint articles was granted by Sage, Inc.

Conversational Beginnings. . . .

The splinter in your eye is the best magnifying glass.
—Adorno, *Minima Moralia*

In putting together Dancing the Data *and the associated CD,* Dancing the Data Too, *we hope to provide an intertextual splinter that will engage and capture the imaginative eye of the reader and spark a debate about the significance and value of using artistic forms to (re)present educational research.*

PART ONE

Dance and Theater Data

CHAPTER 1

Educational Research and Intertextual Forms of (Re)Presentation

The Case for Dancing the Data[1]

CARL BAGLEY AND MARY BETH CANCIENNE

Interpretive Context

In 1997 we participated, along with academics from a range of disciplines and universities, in a session at the annual conference of the American Educational Research Association (AERA), at which an ethnographic data-set on marital relations was represented through music, art, poetry, drama, and dance. The research for the data-set had been conducted by researchers from Brigham Young University, and the findings in the form of both interview transcripts and reports had been sent to (re)presenters with backgrounds in various artistic forms. The data-set was subsequently (re)presented in these forms at a conference session, discussed, and evaluated . . .

Although we welcomed the opportunity to explore the use of intertextual (re)presentations, the improvised dance representation in which we participated was perceived by us, other dance (re)presenters, and the audience, as one of the more difficult and challenging textual forms.

One of the main reasons for this was the amount of time the dance (re)presenters had to prepare for the performance compared to the other artists. Whereas the other (re)presenters "had months to ruminate over the data," the person asked to choreograph the data "pulled out" at the last moment. The session organizers were therefore left with the dilemma of either excluding dance or trying to get something together with *two days'* notice. The decision to proceed with the dance resulted in two (re)presenters (including one of us—Mary Beth) being identified and asked if they could put together an improvised performance based on the data. This they did by "pulling in" several individuals from the audience (including one of us—Carl). Another of the "volunteer" dance (re)presenters with a background in the performing arts remarked on the process and experience in the following terms:

> I was dragged out of the audience last night to take this risk and it was a little wild. . . . I was concerned because it was just thrown out there. After I did it I kind of said, "How did I feel about that?" Not only did we have an obligation to the people we represent, we have an obligation to the art. What we do as an artist takes a lot of practice and to just throw something out there—with some people who have no expertise in the medium—and say this represents qualitative research in an artistic form—I don't know if it does much service to the art form.

A dance educator present at the performance reiterated the danger:

> One of the problems we have had in the dance world is being trivialized and the assumption that you can throw together a dance in two days or two minutes is very problematic. Watching it last night I thought this is so stereotypical, what are these people doing, it trivializes the art form and doesn't speak well for the dance profession.

I *(voice of Mary Beth)* expressed similar concerns:

> I've never done improvisation in front of an audience before. To see the dance trivialized was very painful for me and it was something I didn't realize was going to happen until I was doing it. I am glad I had the experience but I wanted more time to read and choreograph the data.

One of the main things we both took away from the experience, and one that came through strongly from the audience at the evaluation session, could be summarized as a series of unmet obligations arising from the trivialization of the dance performance. All the (re)presenters believed that in interpreting the data-set they had a series of obligations. They felt they had an obligation to the respondents who participated in the research, the researcher who conducted the research, the audience who attended the performance, the art form used for the (re)presentation, to themselves as artists. On each of these levels they considered—due to the way in which the dance performance had been planned and executed—that they had failed.

Sharing these concerns, yet still committed to what we saw as "ground-breaking" work, we decided to develop our own "dancing the data" project. We would reflect critically on the experience, allowing more time and planning to go into a dance performance, and thereby hope to do greater justice to the art form and its potential.

In order to accomplish this task we decided to take educational data collected by one of us (Carl), and have it (re)interpreted and (re)presented as a choreographed performance by the other (Mary Beth), who had a background in the performing arts. The work from which the performance emanated was an analysis of research data from a recently completed, large-scale, general research study into school choice and education policy conducted in the U.K. (Woods, Bagley, & Glatter, 1998). The particular data-set used for the performance concerned the impact of school choice on families whose children had special educational needs (Bagley & Woods, 1998). The venue we selected for the performance was the annual meeting of the AERA in 1998.

Choreographic Process

Carl's Voice. . . . . .

We agreed from the outset that Mary Beth—with her background in the performing arts—would take sole responsibility for choreographing the performance. I knew this to be the right course of action, not least because I knew nothing about choreography, movement, or dance. In terms of supplying Mary Beth with a data-set to choreograph, I selected ten in-depth interviews which I felt broadly reflected the range of parental experiences I had encountered during the fieldwork. I also forwarded an academic paper that outlined the educational policy context and had *in part* drawn on these interviews in its analysis of school choice and special educational needs. Nevertheless, this surrendering of the data-set—my data-set—necessitated a degree of confidence and trust in the professional competency of Mary Beth. I was particularly concerned about my responsibility/obligations to the voices and experiences of my respondents and believed that these should not be trivialized in the way I had seen happen at AERA. I was—to be totally honest—also concerned about my own professional reputation. Putting together the "dancing the data" project was not the same as volunteering at the last minute to perform an improvised dance routine. This would be something I would have co-ownership of and co-responsibility for. So if it went wrong it was my reputation and Mary Beth's on the line. Mary Beth was aware of my concerns and it was reassuring to know that she felt the same way. In fact these mutually held feelings strengthened our professional commitment to the task.

In practical day-to-day terms it was Mary Beth as sole choreographer who, in scripting the performance and (re)presenting it, had to engage with the whole range of pressures emanating from the different obligations we each felt we had.

Mary Beth's Voice. . . . . .

I found the choreographic process to be much more time-consuming and traumatic than I had imagined. A preliminary difficulty arose from the fact that the educational system upon which the data-set was grounded was culturally unfamiliar to me. The initial stages of the choreographic process therefore involved a series of transatlantic telephone calls and frequent e-mails between the two of us to clarify the general educational policy context and the meaning of the written text. For example, I would ask Carl "What are local education authorities and what do they do?" *and* "Are your secondary schools like our middle schools?" In addition, the specific policy relating to special educational needs threw up a whole range of different points needing clarification.

I read and reread the ten interview transcripts in order to become familiar with the meaning and feeling of the words. As I progressed, the words began to evoke strong visual metaphoric images. This process was repeated with the reading of the academic paper. It was apparent to me from these preliminary readings that the most evocative passages highlighted in the transcripts were also frequently used in the academic paper. I therefore decided to make aspects of the academic paper the main focus for the choreographed performance.

Moreover, as the "voices" of parents "speaking out" from the paper (and transcripts) were very strong and powerful I felt that the performance should encompass words as well as movement. I believed that this combination would have the added advantage of grounding the performance piece in a way that would enable the audience to engage with the research topic more directly and analytically.

I considered it equally important for the topic of SEN to be deeply embedded and yet highly visible in the performance. In terms of the choreography I decided that interpretation would tend toward the "literal" and "more obvious" rather than the aesthetic and more avant-garde—the use of movement to (re)present data being sufficiently innovative and pioneering.

I wanted to find literal movements that would reinforce and emphasize the emotional tone of the written text. The purpose of these movements was to bring the text to life in ways that the reading of it could not. There would however be variation within the literal interpretation. I still had numerous choreographic choices to make even after I had decided that the performance should be literal. For example, as we show below in the performance, when a parent states that his or her child can barely write, I do not use my hand; instead, I use my right foot to write a name on the floor. The literal idea of writing is thus evoked but is represented in a nonliteral sense for artistic affect. Similarly, I, as performer, decided not to portray English accents. My performance voices were all to be spoken in my authentic voice as choreographer/dancer. This was done because of my self-acknowledged artistic limitations, being unable to portray accents and not wanting to end up sounding like a female version of Dick Van Dyke's character in Mary Poppins!

During further detailed readings of the academic paper, I circled the action verbs, adjectives, and adverbs of the parents' utterances that were quoted in the paper. I then gave each of the parents' voices an organizing theme that corresponded to the research paper's main findings, such as; limited information, stress and trauma, negotiation, fact-finding exercise, going to school, headteacher's speech, child's friends, and school as a happy place.

In keeping with my desire to offer a literal choreography, I believed the inclusion of the researcher's voice from the paper would further help to ground the performance for the audience. It would provide a more authoritative analytical context and a vocal bridge between the themes as they were uncovered and portrayed in the words and movement of parental voices. The researcher's voice in representing the main findings from the study became an important organizing feature of the performance. It not only provided context but also helped shape timing and delivery.

I subsequently excerpted a statement of the main findings from the academic paper and placed these findings—to be expressed as the researcher's voice—before each of the parents' voices. I decided that the order of the performance (guided by the organizing themes) would move from the researcher's voice to the voices of the parents and continue sequentially in that format. As written papers have headings to guide the reader as to the argument being constructed, so I was striving for "a performance syntax the audiences could understand as easily as they understand the syntax of scholarly papers, whether written or read out" (McCall, Becker, & Meshajian, 1990, p. 123).

I then tape-recorded the sequencing of words and played the tape back to myself in the car while traveling to and from college. This helped me to memorize the lines and to visualize choreographic possibilities while listening to the words. After visualizing several images of possible movements, I went into a dance studio to rehearse possible movements with words, the synthesis of words and movement leading to a reworking of the original images and ideas.

Both male and female voices were to be vocalized through the female voice of the performer with a change of position on stage denoting that a different respondent was speaking. "He" and "she" as gender-specific words were to be used to indicate that the children of the parents were both male and female. I would also portray both the voice of the researcher and the parental voices of the respondents.

Eventually, having reached a point at which I was professionally satisfied with my work, I previewed the performance to faculty members and students from the Curry School of Education at the University of Virginia.

The sequence of choreographed moves I performed did not resemble ballet, modern, tap, or jazz dance; the moves were more like a one-person simplistic or minimalist movement/theatrical sideshow, juxtaposing abstract and more modern dance movements with theatrical and literal movements. For instance, the dance was more abstract when I moved without using voice. This was usually demonstrated after the voice of the researcher identified a theme in the research data, each theme in the performance representing a vignette. At this time, I interpreted the theme by using abstract movements and then slowly integrated these movements with the voices of the participants. At other times, I emphasized the researcher's theme by using movement and voice simultaneously, at which time the performance became more theatrical.

Dance in the performance moves beyond the actual interviews and takes creative license. This is done for purposes of putting old information in a new light and creating a new interpretation, different from the old. It would be absurd to suggest that when Carl was interviewing parents concerning school choice that these parents were dancing. While the movements are motivated by the words of the participants and the researcher, I, the choreographer, undertook an artistic endeavor, created image in motion, and juxtaposed these images with the words of the participants. One of the many questions that I ask as the choreographer interpreting the data is: if thoughts and feelings were imagined through movement, what would they look like?

Feedback from the preview was extremely positive. However, one audience member suggested that the researcher, since he would be present at the AERA conference and "could read out his words in his own authentic voice," should play himself. The idea was therefore generated that Carl should participate directly in the choreographic staging of the performance.

In considering this suggestion I gave careful thought to the task Carl would be assigned and whether he could undertake it without compromising the standard of the performance. The risk of including someone without a background in the performing arts was, given the straightforward—albeit important—nature of the task, outweighed by the benefits of having his authentic voice/self in the performance.

It was not possible for me to relay this decision to Carl, as he was on vacation. Consequently, it was not until 11 o'clock on the night before the AERA presentation that I informed him of my decision to include him in the performance, and presented him with a set of scripted cue cards from which I wanted him to read.

Carl's Voice. . . . . .

I must admit that I greeted her decision to include me in the performance with a degree of hesitancy and trepidation. I realized that until that point I had managed to disengage myself and stand back from all the pressures and obligations that Mary Beth as choreographer had had to deal with. I thus found myself in the lobby of the San Diego Marriott Hotel at the eleventh hour (literally and metaphorically), confronted with a series of questions. Was it the right decision? Could I do it? Would I spoil the performance? Would I let

Mary Beth down if I didn't get it right? Did we have enough time to rehearse?

After some discussion (and several beers!) I decided to trust Mary Beth's professional judgment and confidence in me. Subsequently, that evening and into the early hours of the next day we ran through the performance and then rehearsed it again twice before the actual performance. We were both satisfied—even if I remained somewhat apprehensive—that the performance with both of us in it would work . . .

The Performance

Scene: The audience, approximately 50 people, sits in five rows facing a space which has been cleared for the performance and which will act as an improvised stage. The two performers face the audience. Performer 1 (Carl) sits at the back left-hand side of the stage. Performer 2 (Mary Beth) stands upright center stage.

Performer 1 (reading from cue cards):

"The knowledge of parents of their child's special educational needs remained relatively limited and unclear."

Performer 2:

Standing in the front left-hand corner of the stage, mimes opening a book using hands and says, "I know my child is poor at reading." *Walking to the back right-hand corner of the stage, mimes writing a name with her foot, then looks up and says,* "I know my child can't really write." *Walking to the right front hand corner of the stage paces back and forth and then places her right hand on the right-hand side of her face and says,* "But to be honest, I really don't know what ALL *(emphasis)* my child's needs are when looking for a school."

Performer 1 (reading from cue cards):

"Parents were placed in the awkward position of having to express a preference for a secondary school without knowing the outcome of the child's review, often without assistance from the local education authority."

Performer 2:

Spins round and round and falls to the floor contorting her body and says, "I don't know which way to turn. I don't know which way to turn." *The narrative is then divided, juxtaposing the voice of the parents (on the left side of the stage) and the voice of the local education authority (on the right side of the stage). Speaking in the voice of the local education authority, the performer stands straight, looks stern, and in a deep monotonous voice says, facing left as if to the parent,* "We notice you haven't sent your form back in," *and then, moving to the other side of the room and in the voice of the parent, says,* "No, because you are supposed to be giving me help." *As she says these words, with frustration she stabs one fist in the air and then the other.*

Walking to the other side of the stage, her manner becomes more controlled as she says, "The final decision is yours." *She then walks, stamping her feet as she returns to the back left-hand side of the stage. She faces the audience and says,* "I am annoyed that I didn't get any consultation over what school to send him. I mean I was bitter." *She walks forward,* "I am still very, very bitter." *She then makes two fists and moves them from chest level to the top of her forehead and concludes,* "I'm livid, never mind bitter."

Performer 1 (reading from cue cards):

"The middle class parents tended to be the ones who had spent most time in planning and preparing for a school visit and making a choice."

Performer 2:

Repetitively moving her arms and legs back and forth in a stiff, machine-like pattern, in a monotone robot-like voice, she says, "I conducted a fact-finding exercise. I phoned up all the schools before I visited them, drew up a short list, prepared a set of questions, then visited the school with my child during school hours."

Performer 1 (reading from cue cards):

"One of the main reasons given by the interviewees for choosing a school was the overall philosophy and commitment of the school towards special educational needs."

Performer 2:

(In responding to the statement, the words and movement seek to reflect the perspectives of two parents who attend open evenings at different schools.) Walking to the right-hand side of the stage and speaking on behalf of one parent she lifts her arms into a V-shaped pose while saying, "We went to the head teacher's speech and all he went on about was attainment levels." *Symmetrically lowers her arms stiffly, stopping at different points to represent high, medium, and low attainment levels. She stops the movement and says,* "Non-achievers would be lost." *She drops to the floor on one knee, head faced down, pauses, then raises her head to speak to the audience,* "Our son is a difficult student because he's got poor concentration. We were looking at what was best for him. It just seemed that they were only interested in the kids who were academic and those that are not they don't want to know that sort of thing." *She then lowers her head and pauses.*

Standing she walks to the other side of the stage. As she walks she faces the audience and says, "The head teacher in his speech said what the school had was equality of opportunity, equality for everybody." *As she finishes the sentence she slowly bends her knees and sits on the floor. Cupping her hands out in front of her she stretches them out to her sides and raises them slowly until the palms touch above her head. She then raises her voice and with a big smile says,* "And I like that."

Performer 1 (reading from cue cards):

"An important concern for parents was their child's happiness."

Performer 2:

Jumps, leaps, turns, skips, and kicking her legs side to side says, "If they are happy they will settle quicker and they will be more willing to do work." *Finishing the sentence she turns sideways, bends her knees slightly, and raises her shoulders tightly into her neck to show tension. She continues, speaking with difficulty,* "If you have got a child that is unhappy they get all tensed-up and stressed-out and will struggle."

Releasing the neck position slowly she says, "He's very timid, but he's full of beans *(she jumps and hops around the stage)* and *(standing still facing the audience with arms wide open, smiling)* the school needs to reflect that."

Reflections

For both of us the opportunity to experiment and pioneer intertextual forms of (re)presentation within the academy was a point of immense personal satisfaction and achievement. The refereed acceptance and staging by AERA of our "paper" as a live performance rather than as a traditional printed text was we believe an important step forward in creating a space for the expression of different intertextual forms in educational research, a space we believe is important for establishing the legitimacy of intertextual forms of (re)presentation (see below under outcome for how we believe this step might be consolidated).

The experience, however, of staging the performance highlighted for us the practical and logistical constraints on the use of non-print-based textual forms. At one level these difficulties relate to the very pragmatic problem of finding an appropriate arena in which to stage the performance, in an academy geared to receiving bounded representational forms. While these difficulties can relate to many intertextual forms of representation, we believe them to be particularly evident in the case of a textual form that encompasses movement. For example, prior to the performance we visited the conference room to see if a suitable space in which to speak and move was available. The room was relatively small and had been arranged for a traditional paper presentation, with rows of seats for the audience facing a set of tables and chairs for presenters and discussants alongside an overhead projector and screen. It was therefore necessary for us to rearrange the room in order to create a space for the movement. This having been achieved we left the room, returning 30 minutes later (and 10 minutes before the performance) to discover that in the interim the conference organizers had returned the room to its original layout. Consequently, prior to embarking on the performance and already somewhat nervous and apprehensive about what we were about to attempt, we found ourselves once again rearranging the room as the audience arrived.

This practical difficulty alludes in part to a larger problem concerning the existing culture of the educational academy and its emphasis on the need to formally present papers and establish a published research record based on printed textual forms. In such a culture the spaces and scholarly recognition available and afforded to academics working in mixed genres (Geertz, 1983) is restricted. As Eisner (1999), contributing to an article aptly entitled "A Vision for Educational Research and the American Educational Research Association in the 21st Century" observes, "Because some work cannot be assessed through conventional criteria, there is sometimes a tendency to dismiss it because it does not model traditional canons" (p. 34).

Equally, in writing this paper we are well aware of the potential paradox in advocating words and movement as text and the practical necessity of presenting our case here in print-based form. In doing so we find ourselves asking to what extent does the reader of this paper need to *see* the performance to gather its real impact and significance (McCall et al., 1990). And how do we bridge that gap?

One possible solution to this dilemma resides in the increasing educational role afforded to the use of multimedia. The emergence of on-line journals might make a cross-fertilization of representational genres, which encompass combinations of text as print, image, voice, and movement, increasingly possible. The future availability of alternative forms of publication will nevertheless need to be matched by changes in the culture of the academy in the ways in which unbounded forms of intertextual representation are perceived and judged. Possibly, "the criteria to be applied to any form of work should be guided by the features of the work itself" (Eisner, 1999, p. 34).

Carl's Voice. . . . . .

In terms of my own personal reflections on the process, I found that being able to actively contribute to the performance challenged me and pushed forward the boundaries of what I considered myself capable and how I saw myself as a researcher.

It also gave me an enormous amount of self-satisfaction to see my research performed live. In watching Mary Beth perform I remember thinking wryly, "so this is how playwrights must feel on a first night." Perhaps these feelings were accentuated because I liked what Mary Beth had done with my work and the fact that it was well received by the audience. Certainly, I felt that my obligations to myself as researcher and to the respondents had been met. In addition, as I had performed the piece without any mistake I felt my obligations to Mary Beth as friend, choreographer, and performer had been satisfied.

The performance, while not changing my understanding of the data-set, did allow me to see it and it to touch me in different ways. It could thus be said to have added new dimensions rather than new understandings. For example, Mary Beth's metaphoric interpretations relating to the emotions of parents in showing their stress and trauma by mimicking the *walking of a tight-rope* and the figurative depiction of school choice as a fact-finding exercise related to a *machine in motion* supplied a live, visual, immediate, and emotional re-creation and rereading of my written text. For me the kinesthetic energy of the live performance gave the text a lifelike dimension and lifted the experiences and voices of the participants off the printed page. In so doing it enhanced my appreciation of the power of the genre of movement and dance.

Mary Beth's Voice. . . . . .

The opportunity to represent the piece textually as words and movement created a space which I could make use of and in which to build on existing interests, aptitudes, and skills that in an educational research context I feel have been hitherto underdeveloped and underutilized.

This opportunity, however, raised another issue in my mind concerning the limitations and viability of working intertextually. If, for example, I had no background in performing arts, would the performance have been possible? Indeed, should it even be attempted? Do you need to be a poet to (re)present data as poetry or a dramatist to (re)present data as a play? Possibly in reflecting on these questions we are returned to Eisner's (1997) notion of the "interpretive context," to the need for self-reflexive practice (p. 9), and to what we as researchers perceive to be our responsibilities and obligations.

From the standpoint of a dancer, having the opportunity to work with the data-set over a prolonged period of time—unlike my earlier experience at AERA—enabled me "to do justice to it" as an artist. In this way I was able to ensure that the performance did not trivialize the art form and did satisfy my obligations to the respondents, the researcher, myself, and the audience.

The experience did change my understanding of the data. Getting to know the stories of each of the 10 participants and creating visual pictures and movements to interpret these stories helped me to understand an aspect of educational policy in another country and to engage with the complex and difficult lives of parents of students with special educational needs. For me the act of choreographing the performance brought me into the research. In effect the experience moved me from a standpoint outside the data-set to a standpoint within it.

In analyzing the research data for (re)presentation I found it necessary to reflect in greater depth on the experiences, voices, meanings, and understandings in the data. Similar consideration had to be given to the choice of emphasis, pace, and movement. The process thus necessitated for me (and Carl) a renewed analytical reading of the data (McCall et al., 1990) and required "new ways of seeing" the data for its (re)presentation (Eisner, 1997). In this respect it uncovered the ways in which data analysis and data representation are inextricably tied together, and highlighted the potential for unbounded representations to "escape from analytical perspectives that have become stereotypes and stale" (Coffey & Atkinson, 1996, p. 13).

Shared Voice. . . . . .

The rereading highlighted for both of us the dominance and omniscience of the analytic voice within the bounded print-based text of the academic paper and importantly afforded an opportunity for its deconstruction and repositioning. In "dancing the data" we were able to facilitate a movement away from and disruption of the monovocal and monological nature of the voice in the print-based paper. Through a choreographed performance we were provided with an opportunity to encapture the multivocal and dialogical, as well as to cultivate multiple meanings, interpretations, and perspectives that might engage the audience in a recognition of textual diversity and complexity (Dwyer, 1977, 1979; Holquist, 1990; Allan, 1994). The data as words and movement in freeing "representation from its descriptive intent" (Constas, 1999, p. 39) could thus be considered evocative rather than "denotative" facilitating a notion of "productive ambiguity" (Eisner, 1997).

We feel the use of words and movement made the content of the data presentable and discernible to the audience in a way that could not have been achieved by a more bounded representational form. Certainly, the performance enabled "information about mood and emotions, as well as events and attitudes" to be portrayed (McCall et al., 1990, p. 122). For example, the use of strong facial and body movements accompanying the parental voice helped, as one audience member stated, "to bring to life" the range of emotional feelings of anger, frustration, despair, joy, and happiness experienced by parents of students with special needs. For other audience members the more literal interpretation of movement and words highlighted the emotionally fraught traumatic world of parents and juxtaposed it with the unemotional, bureaucratic, authoritative world of the local education authority and the voices of its officials. As an audience member said, "being able to watch you change your movements as different voices spoke really let me see and feel as well as hear the different experiences of parents."

Another audience member observed that the choreographic pattern of the movement and voices varied. He noted that sometimes there was movement for 30 seconds before speech and at other times speech right before movement. The audience member said it was easiest for him to make the connection between the words and movement when the movement followed the words. In effect, when he could see "more literally" what was being interpreted he could connect with the written text, understand the major themes of the research study, and feel the emotions of the participants.

On a more critical note, one audience member said that while she thought the performance was "emotional and informative" for the audience and a "creative and imaginative" endeavor for the choreographer, she would still rather have read the written text. In reading rather than "seeing and hearing" she believed she would have had a greater opportunity "to imagine the participants' voices and meanings." For her the performance did not require her to be creative, as the choreographer had already done this for her. In this sense the performance, while touching her emotionally and informatively, hindered rather than facilitated the use of her imagination.

In reflecting on the experience we believe the use of words and movement revealed itself to have the evocative potential and power to engage and capture the audience and ourselves, to enable them and us to gain on multiple levels access to an understanding of the lives of parents with children with special educational needs, and hopefully to ensure that we and the audience empathize more readily with the personal and educational situations these parents face (Eisner, 1997).

Furthermore, it can be hoped that in engendering a sense of empathy the performance, in terms of Denzin's (1997) "sixth moment in the history of ethnography" may have done more than "awaken moral sensibilities": it may have contributed to the development of an intertextual representational genre which is able to "move the other and the self to action" (p. xxi). In essence it had the potential for engendering a notion of praxis in us all.

Notes

1. In this chapter we are viewing not only printed text but also dance (more accurately, spoken words and movement) as textual forms. Consequently as we show and explore the interplay and interrelationship between these texts, we believe the work needs to be seen and described as *intertextual*. For those—like us—committed to exploring an unbounded methodological approach to data (re)presentation we feel this to be a more discursively accurate and meaningful description than the more commonly used notion of "alternative forms of representation." We believe the use of the word "alternative" implies and reinforces bounded notions of (re)presentation in which text as print is able to discursively maintain its dominant and mainstream position at the centre of the academy while simultaneously situating and confining other textual forms to the periphery. We therefore offer the term intertextual as a way forward, to facilitate conversations between equal partners about the strengths and weaknesses of using different textual forms to (re)present data. This chapter is an abridged version of an article that appears in *Qualitative Inquiry*, 7(2), pp. 221–237.

2. For a more thorough report of this, see Morgan, Mienczakowski, & Smith, 2000, pp. 172–176.

3. These edited data are drawn from an exploration of the experiences of road traffic accident victims and the perusal of compensation claims through legal processes. Working with a professional psychologist frequently paid by legal services and/or insurance companies to assess psychological impacts related to recovery processes, this excerpt examines the roles of medical professionals and insurance representatives in compensation claims.

References

Allan, S. (1994). When discourse is torn from reality: Bakhtin and the principle of chronotopicity. *Time and Society, 3*, 193–218.

Bagley, C., & Woods, P. A. (1998). School choice, markets and special educational needs. *Disability and Society, 13*(5).

Becker, H. S., McCall, M. M., Morris, L. V., & Meshejian, P. (1989). Theatres and communities: Three scenes. *Social Problems, 36*(2), 93–98.

Coffey, A., & Atkinson, P. (1996). *Making sense of qualitative data. Complementary research strategies.* London: Sage.

Constas, M. A. (1999). Deciphering postmodern educational research. *Educational Researcher, 27*(9), 36–41.

Denzin, K. (1997). *Interpretive ethnography: Ethnographic practice for the 21st century.* London: Sage.

Dwyer, K. (1977). On the dialogic of fieldwork. *Dialectical Anthropology, 2,* 143–151.

Dwyer, K. (1977). On the dialogic of ethnology. *Dialectical Anthropology, 4,* 205–224.

Eisner, E. W. (1997). The promise and the perils of alternative forms of data representation. *Educational Researcher, 26*(6), 4–10.

Eisner, E. W. (1999). "The vision thing": Educational research and AERA in the 21st century—part 5: A vision for educational research and the American Educational Research Association in the 21st century. *Educational Researcher, 27*(9), 34.

Geertz, C. (1983). *Local knowledge: Further essays in interpretative anthropology.* New York: Basic Books.

Holquist, M. (1990). *Dialogism: Bakhtin and his world.* London: Routledge.

McCall, M. M., Becker, H. S., & Meshajian, P. (1990). Performance science. *Social Problems, 37*(1), 117–132.

Woods, P. A., Bagley, C., & Glatter, R. (1998). *School choice and competition: Markets in the public interest?* London: Routledge.

CHAPTER 2

Bodydance: Enfleshing Soulful Inquiry through Improvisation

CELESTE SNOWBER

Introduction

In expanse and contraction the dancer can say it all, the ecstasy and grief of living in this multiple, complex world with all its amazement and terror. The art of dance improvisation as performative inquiry explores knowledge through the body, using its capacity to release the imagination, to uncover places of discovery, surprise, mystery, and wonder. In my work I integrate the art of autobiographical narrative and dance, to develop a series of performances that become narratives of the body. These performances focus on the theme of multiplicity as a way of examining the value of our multiple lives, roles, and responsibilities and multiple ways of knowing. Central to this is the art of improvisation, which I use with my students as a studio for research, creating a paradigm for theorizing with the body. Parker Palmer has eloquently said, "we teach who we are" (1998, p. 2), and the arts in inquiry allow us to access the crevices of our souls and bring the fullness of our humanity to the process of being, living, knowing, and teaching. Improvising alerts one to the present, and it is often in this space of not knowing what may happen next that one learns ways to develop a physicality of knowing—a thinking on the feet. The body has the capacity to be a huge teacher in our lives, and this chapter shows how the data of the body can be a place where the soul can sing and the bones dance.

Central to this research is a methodology that draws on phenomenological curriculum research, narrative inquiry, autobiographical writing, and performative inquiry. I will expand on a theory of embodiment that supports a poetic rendering of knowledge and articulates text in physically provocative ways. I draw on theorists and writers who have forged poetic ways of writing the embodied self into being, for example, Cixous (1993), Aoki (1993), Griffin (1995), Abram (1996), and Brandt (1996). I am also influenced by feminist epistemology, which provides a foundation for the merging of many worlds and fosters methods of research that bridge the gap between private and public, emotion and cognition, theory and life, ecstatic and rational, body and mind. Julia Kristeva (1980) argues that we can and must recover the capacity to question and wonder, and for me the integration of dance improvisation into inquiry is a methodology of dancing the questions into wonder.

I will look at data in the form of body data and body knowledge. The data of my research will be enfleshed in the physical nuances of lived experience. The theme of multiplicity is central to this research, both in my own work as a researcher/artist/educator and in the lives of my students in a faculty of education. My research has drawn upon a variety of conversations with teachers, student teachers, and undergraduate and graduate students in education on the notion of living multiple lives. This methodology reframes inquiry as a place of spiritual formation and sees it as a journey into ourselves—an inquiry of body and soul, a place where a space is opened up for the possibilities of inquiry to be transformative.

It is important to note that this research is done within the scope of an understanding of the "lived curriculum" as opposed to the curriculum-as-plan. The lived curriculum characterizes what takes place in the margins of learning, where both child and adult interconnect with the world and the physical self. It is here where the nuances of gesture, smell, touch, sound, and sight shape us and inform our lives. It is into these margins that this chapter travels, the margins of sensuous knowledge, where all of life, and not just what takes place within the walls of the classroom, can be seen as a place for learning and wonder. The walls are extended into the halls of all aspects of life. The theme of "multiplicity" is a thread that holds together the variety of our ways of living and perceiving the world. The notion of multiplicity is also woven into the use of metaphor, both in narrative and performative inquiry. Ted Aoki (1997) expands on this place of metaphor, which has been so central to phenomenological curriculum research. He speaks of "dwelling in the midst of doubling of live(d) experiences," in conjunction with narrating our lived experience, in a place for the recovery of the past as well as the production of the present. This place, he continues, is "dwelling in the midst of ambivalence and ambiguity," replacing the Modernist binaries of "Either-Or," and providing a space for dynamic possibility (p. 3). Dance becomes this place of dynamic possibility where the invisible and visible become partners.

Body Data

As researchers and artists we are familiar with the process of observation. We observe the world keenly and attend to the fine points of words. We collect data. Yet as human beings we constantly receive bodily data, visual data, auditory data, and tactile data. In fact, there is so much of it, we are often overwhelmed by the sheer physical overload of outside stimulation. There is an assault on the senses that we have often learned to tune out. On the other hand, there is a place for noting more intensely the bodily nuances and cues that come to us each day. The tension in our shoulders, the flurry in our chests, the grimace on our faces, the joy rising up in our torsos, the sense of expectancy we feel when there is a new possibility. Much of our relating in the world is experienced through our body, yet seldom do we take this as a serious place of study. But we understand viscerally the language of gesture, posture, and nuances of bodily expression. It is second nature, as natural to us as brushing our teeth. As dancers and performers we learn to find these places in our bodies and skillfully and artfully learn to expand the knowledge of the data our bodies give us. It is essential to the choreographic process. When is it best to turn, fall, stop, create wideness with our bodies, change rhythm, contract, expand, curl in a ball, or reach for the sky? The body has its reasons and the choreographer crafts these into art. Or as the great modern dance pioneer, Martha Graham, says in her autobiographical work, *Blood Memory*, "Movement never lies. It is a barometer telling the state of the soul's weather to all who can read it" (1991, p. 4). Body data therefore is the information that occurs in the present moment, the immediate present-time, the ways we experience information through our bodies (Porter & Winton-Henry, 1997, p. 25). Listening to our own body data is just the beginning of probing the possibilities of a physicality of knowing.

Our bodies have a memory. Of course, this is substantiated in a variety of fields within both the human sciences and the biological sciences, as well by as body practitioners working in the fields of dance therapy, physiotherapy, and other body-oriented disciplines. However, novelists and poets more provocatively state embodied memory. It is not uncommon for us to recall a memory through a smell, a return to our childhood geography, or to be reminded of someone we loved through a familiar gesture. We are awakened to memory through our bodies, the reminder of the smell of the sea, fresh raspberries in jam, the feel of an oak table, or the gesture of a closed fist or an open palm. Alice Miller recalls this well when she says, "The truth about our childhood is stored up in our body, and although we can repress it, we can never alter it" (Miller, 1984, p. 316). One can have all the analytical data about the relationship between memory and the body, but the poet captures glimpses of the power of a physical remembrance in an intimate encounter with the other. Beautifully captured in a poem by Anne Michaels (1997, p. 46), bodily knowing reaches our souls:

> Fingers have a memory,
> to read the familiar braille of another's skin.
> The body has a memory:
> the children we make,
> places we've hurt ourselves,
> sieves of our skeletons in the fat soil.
> No words mean as much as a life.
> Only the body pronounces perfectly
> the name of another.

Attention to the body gives us the space to open new rooms, for others and for the passion living inside us.

Body Narratives

As a writer and dancer I have combined the art of autobiographical narrative and dance, developing a choreographic process called "body narratives." Largely using the art of improvisation, I repeatedly dance the narratives of my own life and the questions and responses from my students as a way of accessing, developing, chiseling, editing, and creating material. As I listen to my own body data, I am given the impetus for the paint on my canvas, the notes of my instrument, the sounds in my flesh. I draw on all the movement language available to me in my body: the contractions of Graham technique, the flowing movement of Jose Limon, the extensions of ballet, the groundedness of African dance, the subtle hand gestures of Indian classical dance, the abandonment of dance in prayer, and the expansion of ordinary human gesture. The forms I know so well in my body are in some ways dormant until the body data summons up the kind of expressivity I need to communicate the multiplicity of my own life. Emotions and experiences embedded in my professional and personal life find form in every extended foot, fall to the ground, leap in the air, contraction in the pelvis. Inner and outer find a marriage through the narrative of flesh and heart.

The main body narrative that I explored during the few months prior to writing this narrative is a piece called "Loosening and Laundry." This dance originated as a narrative piece reflecting the relationship between daily life, teaching, and writing and I developed its form through the relationship between dancing and speaking the narrative. This piece was performed in a variety of venues and is evolving as a place of performative inquiry through my interaction with students, educators, researchers, and audiences. The emergent theme in this work is the paradoxes we hold within us living the multiple roles and responsibilities of our lives.

Dance Improvisation and Performative Inquiry

Dance improvisation is the art of working and playing with movement. It is a way of discovering that which we know and that which we do not know. I do not know how I will integrate the prop of the laundry basket in my body narrative until it is there sitting in front of me on stage. The laundry basket becomes a living partner in this dance; at times I fold it as in a Zen meditation and other times expulse unmatched socks in the confines of space. Through my interaction with it, turning and twirling with it, pushing and pulling it, and at points even sitting and reading in it, my body forms a more tangible relationship with the otherness of my own life. It becomes a recurring point of departure and return, allowing me to explore the unknowable through voice, text, humor, and dance. This concept of exploring what we do not know is central to shifting the paradigm of knowing to not knowing. The word *improvisation* stems from the Latin *improvisus,* which means "unforeseen." The element of surprise, wonder, mystery, and discovery is at the heart of improvisation as the dancer, writer, or artist forms the unformed until that which is invisible becomes visible. Improvisation becomes the act of instantaneously finding fresh movement. One utilizes the elements of design, shape, tempo, directionality, repetition, focus, space, movement qualities, emotive content, conceptual ideas, and philosophical questions as the seeds of creating a dance piece. Improvisation, however, does not excuse poor technique or lack of practice. One cannot have freedom without form, for form does not emerge unless one has gotten messy in the choreographic process. Improvisation is the artistic practice which both reveals and masks at the same time. One does not know what will happen, where he/she will go next in movement, or what word will come up as the body explores the turns and twists of gravity. It is a fertile place where inspiration can not only be born but be nourished. As artists, writers, educators, and researchers, the heart of our work needs inspiration to be fused into our practice. After all, knowledge is essentially a thirst, a desire, a longing sometimes for the intangible. Expressed so beautifully by theologian John O'Donohue (1999), "our desire to know is the deepest longing of the soul; it is a call to intimacy and belonging." He goes on to say that "true knowledge makes us aware of the numinous and awakens desire" (p. 18). The art of improvisation is a place for enfleshing inquiry into a visceral place of continually thirsting for knowledge. I have found several areas that are ripe with insight, and I will elaborate on them: discovery and wonder, surrender and surprise.

Discovery and Wonder

The art of improvisation teaches both my students and me the capacity for discovery and wonder. I have the privilege of teaching dance education classes, where the art of improvisation is fundamental to the class. The community that is formed by a class of 30 adults engaging in the art of dance improvisation is tremendous. Community becomes communion as safe spaces are opened up, validating and affirming the ongoing body narratives of each participant. bell hooks so exquisitely talks of the beauty of sharing one's story: "the longing to tell one's story and the process of telling is symbolically a gesture of longing to recover the past in such a way that one experiences both a sense of reunion and a sense of release" (hooks, 1999, p. 84). To experience this reunion and release in the context of community, story, and dance allows magic to happen and creates what one student called a "garden to cultivate our souls." I offer to you the poem *Dancing Community,* which I wrote for the closing class of one semester and shared as a part of our closing ritual.

Dancing Community

You came
shy, excited, apprehensive,
time unraveled
bodies furled and swayed
our meetings between
breath and play
swings and shapes
skips and sound
soared soul
into the classroom.

A taste of heaven
in the window
of academe.

Dancing in the institution
of higher learning
is unlearning.

To teach children
we must know
how to be/come
children.
Free abandon
baptized imagination
overflowing juices
of art-full living.

The body knows
what it knows—
the exquisite taste
of communion
in dancing community.

The dance
not outside you
but within you
asking to be
birthed and rebirthed
in context of
this wondrous,
sometimes painful
and surprising life.

Know this,
as you dance
and live—
we all go with you.
The dancing community.

The joy of discovery became the heart of what improvisation had to offer in this class and could be transferred to other areas of participants' lives. Imagination is more important than knowledge, as Albert Einstein said, but I would say we need imaginative knowledge where discovery is at the core of our knowing.

Surrender and Surprise

Key to the improvisational process is the development of listening, not only with the mind, but with every cell of the body. This listening entails not only deciding where to let the imagination take one but when to surrender to the right movement, or for that matter, the right word, rhythm, or pause. It is the discipline of knowing when to go with an artistic impulse and when not to go with it. You do not always know where a piece of art will lead you. It has been interesting to me that often the most provocative parts of a book I have written, or dances I have created, are the parts that took me by surprise. My body needs to continue to take me to ways of movement/language which go outside my own predictable vocabulary. I want to be surprised by humor, or find an expansion through my spine, or a new place of stillness that is profoundly alive.

In Western culture we have predominantly thought of education as an accumulation of knowledge. However, this is not the case in all cultures, and Joan Halifax (1999), anthropologist and author, expands on an alternative to this paradigm. She speaks of *initiation* as a place to "plunge inward." She says, "Initiation takes us into the unknown and is grounded in not-knowing" (p. 10). A sense of unknowing is central to the art of improvisation, for when I am engaged in improvisation, I must suspend all that I think, and yet at the same time be able to recall everything that I know in the bodymind. It is going to the edge of the cliff and really seeing that you can fly. Halifax asks the question, "Where are the rituals that open us to not-knowing?" (p. 175). I would suggest that the process of improvisation and creation in all the arts is an embodied ritual which leads us into not-knowing, and ultimately into knowing. Central to "not-knowing" is the element of surprise. Nachmanovitch (1990) in his classic book on improvisation says, "We can depend on the world being a perpetual surprise in perpetual motion, and a perpetual invitation to create" (p. 22). Improvisation is in action, a way to cultivate a listening to surprise. This applies not only to the creative process, but to all of life. Our lives are an artwork in and of themselves, being formed, informed, and transformed in the palette of lived experience. The ways we listen and respond are central to the act of teaching and are the ingredients for good pedagogy and for innovative research. Improvisation is the pilgrimage to release the imaginative possibilities through our whole being. Nachmanovitch goes on to say, "Improvisation is intuition in action, a way to discover the muse and learn to respond to her call" (p. 41).

To take intuition into action, one needs practice. Practice is essential to any skill being developed, honed, and refined. When one thinks of improvisation, one may think of someone engaging in a practice that may not be thoughtful, intentional, or rigorous. It is just the opposite. The imagination is like a muscle, and unless it is utilized consistently it becomes dormant. We need practices in our lives as researchers and educators that provide a verdant ground to let our imaginations soar. I will show how my own performative inquiry has opened up the notion of multiplicity.

Dancing Multiplicity: Reframing Inquiry

It is through dancing body narratives that I have discovered how the theme of multiplicity has informed me for years. These dances continue to integrate my multiple lives, roles, and ways of knowing. We carry worlds within our hearts. The word multiple seems to be foremost in my personal and vocational life, as I have given birth to multiples (twins), am an academic and artist, am a multidisciplinary performer, and teach in an area that draws on multiple intelligences. Feminist writers have argued that the personal is political, and surely our motherhood and fatherhood can inform our scholarship, artistry, and practice. The sheer reality of time constraints has forced me to do many things at the same time: reflect while folding the laundry, read correspondence when my boys are playing at the park, e-mail my colleagues while a son sits on my lap, and referee a fight while having an important conversation. But what is more important to me is the question of how the "otherness" of our lives infiltrates, informs, and possibly transforms our vocational lives, and in particular our lives as educators, artists, and researchers.

As part of the ongoing search for an answer to this question, I chose to dance the narrative I wrote, entitled "Loosening and Laundry." This narrative has room for fluidity as it can incorporate other people's ideas of multiplicity as well. Since I am an improviser, I draw on audiences' experiences/questions and philosophical musings as information with which to create. As I performed this piece in multiple venues, I asked a variety of audiences—including classes of undergraduate students of dance education, communities of preservice teachers, teachers teaching teachers, and colleagues from other educational institutions—their thoughts on multiplicity. At some points I incorporated their responses into the performance as a way of incarnating their reflections, and at other points I used the performance piece as a place to dive deeper into the questions. Each audience brought delightful additions to this piece, both in a concrete way and also in their own critical inquiry. The members of one audience decided to add their own clothing, scarves, hats, or socks, to the laundry piece before I danced in it. In another performance, I felt it necessary to throw the laundry around the room, which raised discussion later about how we are often too tied to certain ideals. In this way I stretch the ways performative inquiry can be utilized, both as a process for excavating information and as a process for reflexivity.

Even though there are points of change in each performance, I find patterns of similarity in the various venues. I continue to begin this piece with abrupt, frenetic movement, flexed feet, and contracted pelvis relaying the energy it takes to live a multiple life. Soon after the initial movement in silence, the narrative commences and I read text and simultaneously dance throughout this ten minute piece. I must listen to the movement that recurs, the places of anchor both in the dance and in my life. Pattern is as exquisite as unpredictability. Both are needed for balance. One movement that recurs is a throwing gesture with forceful clasping and clinging juxtaposed with bringing my arms and palms to my sternum. This rhythmic motion teaches me the nature of the letting go process, being one where I let go and take back, relinquish and retrieve. I do not let go in one sweeping movement, but in a series of culminating motions, which coexist in a long process. In observing this movement I can more clearly inquire into what letting go means, and what I must attend to for my own wholeness. One member of an audience spoke of the impact of this movement, one which stood out for him, and commented that one gesture expressed a strength that possibly hundreds of words would be needed to express. A world in a gesture. This one movement has the capacity to become a strong point for the members of the group to inquire more deeply into the process of letting go in their own lives. As I teach them the movement, they too can viscerally experience what it means to relinquish and take back with the body.

It is important to note that each audience had a different focal point, given their particular school and life experiences. For example, the sheer difference of age between undergraduate students and teachers working with preservice teachers produces a diversity of life experiences, skills, and goals. The particular stages of adulthood are evident whether in young adulthood or midlife issues, both being pertinent to vocational growth. The gift of performative inquiry is to honor all stages of our life as an opening for places of birth.

At this point I would also like to state that dance is an art form which draws on a variety of sensory intelligence, kinesthetic, visual, dramatic, musical, and poetical. Primary to dance are images, and "images reveal that we are holographic creatures living multiple stories" (Allen, 1995, p. 110). Artistic form is representative of multiplicity in and of itself, and images have a huge capacity to guide us through our multiple realities of past and present, personal and professional, mythic and spiritual.

The metaphor that best helps me describe the importance of integrating dance in inquiry is that of a prism. Many times it is hard to understand how the multiple lives we have fit together, how they tie into one another and inform our different roles. The process of dancing an audience's views on "multiplicity" lends itself to reframing experience and values in fresh ways. It is no different from painting a picture and standing back and being able to see the image in a whole new light. This reexamination of the way multiplicity is woven into life allows for a new place honoring the complexity of our lives. For example, one teacher commented on how it was seldom appreciated that her personal life should be valued in its relationship to pedagogy. Another teacher noted the way the performance allowed the group to go to another level that they wouldn't have reached before, opening up a space for riskier questions and more vulnerability. The integration of humor in the performance uncovers the possibility of cherishing the humanity we bring to our vocation as teachers and researchers. As I, the performer, share my own story through dance and voice, I open up a place for the audience to share more intimately their own stories and give them permission to access the other parts of themselves. We create and re-create our own stories together, and thus create and re-create our own worlds.

Performative inquiry lends itself to the uncovering of layers of insights. The very reality that there is room for ambiguities allows the space for a continual unfolding of images and thoughts to solidify into a bodily wisdom. Images stay with us, and continue to work on the soul. As the performer, my own reflections continue to form and transform even as I write this piece. I am therefore more and more invited into what it means to "not know" rather than "to know." The more I delve into fleshing inquiry through the body, the more deeply aware I am of the paradoxes resonant within me. The awareness of my own paradoxes through the experience of dancing the notion of multiplicity has prompted me to use this as a starting point for the ongoing work of this piece. I have more recently asked students and teachers I work with to examine the paradoxes in their teaching, living, and researching. What do they have to teach us and how can a deeper understanding of paradox help us to understand the other? I am beginning to think of paradox as "paradoxology"—in praise of paradox. The situations in our lives, even those which are uninvited guests, become fertile spaces for leaning into new questions and possibilities for wonder. If we stay long enough with the places of dissonance, we are broken into crisp ways of seeing and perceiving.

Conclusion

This chapter has sought to explore the relationship between dance improvisation, bodily knowing, and performative inquiry. The very nature of improvisation is one that defies definition, opening up as many questions as it does limits and possibilities. What is clear is that the very nature of improvisation lends itself to the exploration of life's experiences and knowledge in a multifaceted manner. Key to this process is the importance of the invitation to unknowing, rather than knowing. It is in that suspension of knowing that one can see something with alertness, as if seeing for the first time. T. S. Eliot has eloquently stated, "And the end of all our exploring will be to arrive where we started and know the place for the first time" (1944/1972, p. 59). This is the gift and usefulness of bringing the body to the place of inquiry. It is as if we come again and see it for the first time.

References

Abram, D. (1996). *The spell of the sensuous: Perception and language in a more-than-human world.* New York: Pantheon Books.

Allen, P. (1995). *Art is a way of knowing.* Boston: Shambhala.

Aoki, T. (1993). Legitimizing lived curriculum: Towards a curricular landscape of multiplicity. *Journal of Curriculum and Supervision, 8*(3), 255–258.

Aoki, T. (1997). Curriculum as narrative/narrative as curriculum. *Educational Insights* [On-line serial] *4*(1) Available: www.lane.educ.ubc.ca

Brandt, D. (1996). *Dancing naked: Narrative strategies for writing across centuries.* Stratford, Ontario: Mercury Press.

Cixous, H. (1993). *Three steps on the ladder of writing.* New York: Columbia University Press.

Eliot, T. S. (1944/1972). "Little Gidding" in Section V. *Four Quartets.* London: Faber & Faber.

Glazer, S. (Ed.). (1994). *The heart of learning: Spirituality in education.* New York: Jeremy P. Tarcher/Putnam.

Graham, M. (1991). *Blood memory.* New York: Doubleday.

Griffin, S. (1995). *The eros of everyday life: Essays on ecology, gender and society.* New York: Anchor-Doubleday.

Halifax, J. (1999) Learning as initiation: Not-knowing, bearing witness, and healing. In S. Glazer (Ed.), *The heart of learning: Spirituality in education.* New York: Jeremy P. Tarcher/Putnam.

hooks, b. (1999). *Remembered rapture: The writer at work.* New York: Henry Holt & Company.

Kristeva, J. (1980). *Desire in language: A semiotic approach to literature and art.* (T. Gora, A. Jardine, L. & Roudiez, Trans.). New York: Columbia University Press. Michaels, A. (1997). *The weight of oranges/miners pond.* Toronto: McClelland & Stewart.

Miller, A. (1984). *Thou shalt not be aware: Society's betrayal of the child.* New York: Penguin/Meridian.

Nachmanovitch, S. (1990). *Free play: The power of improvisation in life and the arts.* New York: Jeremy P. Tarcher/Pedigree.

O'Donohue, J. (1999). *Eternal echoes: Exploring our yearning to belong.* San Francisco: HarperCollins/Cliff Street Books.

Palmer, P. (1998). *The courage to teach: Exploring the inner landscape of the teacher's life.* San Francisco: Jossey Bass.

Porter, P., & Winton-Henry, C. (1997). *Having it all: Body, mind & spirit together again at last.* Oakland, CA: Wing It! Press.

CHAPTER 3

Seeing Words–Hearing Feelings: Ethnodrama and the Performance of Data

JIM MIENCZAKOWSKI, LYNN SMITH, AND STEVE MORGAN

Performed data has an empathetic power and dimension often lacking in standard qualitative research narratives. Data as performance has a demonstrable potential to construct explanations from within for particular health consumption groups. It also possesses the potential to destabilize sensitivities. To remain true to the informants who contribute data to our research we require a new aesthetic through which we may interpret and consume these research explanations: the ethnodrama.

Gone is the primacy of "artistry." Individual performance is of secondary consequence here—this form of performance is about informants. Informants will be in the audiences. Informants will participate in post-performance discussions about the representations made. What motivates most of these ethnodrama audiences to debate is the performance's content and relation to real health experiences, not its style. Consequently, elements of these performed researches require new artistic understandings, since from the perspective of a person with schizophrenia life itself may not be experienced in a coherent form recognizable to others. Accuracy and credibility are of more import (to health-related audiences) than theatrical traditions and expectations. Our conception of this new aesthetic in the form of the ethnodrama has positively changed the understanding, attitudes, and perceptions of medical practitioners, caregivers, and others toward particular health consumption scenarios.

As visual and performing artists, it often appears, we do not readily ask whether we should be collectively held responsible for the implications of our art—frequently preferring to defer to postmodern conceptions of individuality and a theoretical inability to collectivize or speak on behalf of audiences. So the visual iconoclasm of urine- and feces-filled artworks (for example, those of American artist and photographer Andres Serrano) may be perceived as nothing less than a revision or reinterpretation of age-old themes in the arts. Similarly, the "challenging" nature of alternative forms of performance such as these given by Karen Wakefield's Triangle Theatre Company or artist Damien Hirst's installations and sculptures, which juxtapose conceptions about beauty/decay, order/chaos, life/death, are an obvious attempt to stretch or distort the limitations of communally accepted aesthetic social boundaries or understandings. This is art challenging society. Critical health theater adds a further dimension: performance art targeting sometimes "fragile" audiences.

In this postmodern era it sometimes appears that "actors" revel in a self-imposed duty to unsettle, to provoke, and to contest popularly held values and conceptions. In this manner, Bauman's (2000) vision of the "public space" as becoming "increasingly empty of public issues" (p. 40) is daily more apparent. However, one needs to remember that audiences may also collectively share responses to emotional stimuli (Mienczakowski, Smith, & Sinclair, 1996) and join in what may be described as constructed catharsis. Such may be the case with health theater which predominantly attracts "health audiences", consisting of clients, health care professionals, and associated others (Mienczakowski, 1995, 1996).

Australian government initiatives to provide intervention strategies for designated "at risk" areas such as youth suicide and alcohol and drug use have seen a huge investment in awareness programs. So the "health agenda" has now become a theater agenda of increasing interest to both fringe and professional theater. The artificial division between theater as "art" and theatre as "therapy" is eroding and challenging Western notions of drama as "cultural representation." In the postmodern world, art has become the vehicle for personal expression, comment, and argument in which each individual (Hebdidge, 1988) can take from a piece of art only that which he or she perceives to be true (possibly not sharing the understanding or intent of the artist's innermost motivations). By extension, as observers we are all participating in (visual or performing) art as therapy. We are in effect fulfilling Bauman's (2000) pronouncement that fluid modernity has abandoned the fight for a just society for all, in favor of our individual "right" to do what we will, when we will, with no responsibility for the effects of our actions upon others.

It is this apparent void in terms of communal impact or ethos of public responsibility that our conception of ethnodrama seeks to fill. Ethnodrama performance as a means of demonstrating data, exploring research, and seeking new research values is, thus, in our conception, the construction of a new aesthetic through which the performing arts can make meaningful contributions to human understanding. Ethnodrama's conception is one expression of the steady move toward a broader application of postmodernity's licensing of the uniqueness and authenticity of the individual's interpretations and forms of expression within the sphere of health theater. This shift was alluded to by the late Richard Courtney (1981), who explored the world of drama in therapy (in Schattner & Courtney, 1981) without fully removing the line between aesthetic drama and therapeutic performance work. Much other academic research in areas such as social justice and education has been similarly self-serving rather than widely applicable to others—what we describe as "a sandwich in your own lunch-box" research, which serves your own constructs in the name of the "other."

Through the agency of this chapter we want to prompt a wider debate about both the emancipatory potential of health theater and the ethical quandaries posed for the health agendas of health theater research informants. As health researchers we must be cognizant of the potential impact of our interactions with health care recipients as we gather our data. Simultaneously we seek to promote discussion about the real impact of the collaboratively developed scripts of the ethnodrama report and the ethical and emotional dilemmas experienced when performance groups fail to anticipate the potentially harmful effects on the recovery of clients seated in the audience (Morgan, Rolfe, & Mienczakowski, 1999; Mienczakowski, Smith, & Sinclair, 1996).

To illustrate these concerns, in our text we have included references to performed representations and critical perspectives, in recognition of the validity of our informants' lived experiences as recorded in the verbatim field data collection process. This chapter is thus a reflection of the "seeing words–hearing feelings" approach that we employed. Our methodology ensured the veracity and integrity of our scripts and performances through the inclusion of informants' explanations of their health experiences, be they suicide attempts, cosmetic surgery, rape, or drug and alcohol detoxification processes, and the translation of informants' experiences into the public performance of the resulting ethnodrama texts. In effect, we used good, standard, qualitative ethnographic interview practice and interpretive ethnography reported through the performance of data and data/informant-related scenarios.

Dealing with Health Issues: The Point of Critical Capture

Bauman's (1992) definition of the postmodern condition as "perhaps more than anything else—a state of mind. More precisely—a state of those minds who have the habit (or is it a compulsion?) to reflect upon themselves, to search their own contents and report what they found: the state of mind of philosophers, social thinkers, artists—all those people on whom we rely when we are in a pensive mood or just pause for a moment to find out whence we are moving or being moved" [p. vii, Introduction] is tangentially related to the methodology of ethnodrama. The potential for reflexivity, autonomy, marginalization, and dispossession is the theme underpinning our précis of the health care system and its potential as a form of cartharsis as expressed in our new, qualitative form of experimental theater research. But let us not get carried away here. Avoiding the state of postmodern "self reflexivity and auto-reflection," which might inhibit meaningful action (Hebdidge 1988; McLaren 1995), ethnodrama seeks to turn health care recipients from "the individual de facto" into "the individual de jure" (Bauman, 2000, pp. 40–41).

Applying Blumer's (1976) symbolic interactionist notion of the "looking glass self" in conjunction with the reflexive and collaborative validatory endeavors of the then-experimental health theater advocated by Turner (1986), we are able to create scripts rich with authentic context and meaning. Critical ethnodrama has thus become a qualitative vehicle capable of reaching a wider cross section of the community in a meaningful and accessible way (Morgan & Mienczakowski, 1993). The scripts are consensually constructed with the insight and control of health informants, health agencies, and health professionals. They follow the simple guideline of responding to informants' wishes and needs. They seek to "explain" the worlds of "the other" in the language and words of "the other." We are performing credible scenarios because they are the words, emotions, and actions of those who intimately inhabit those worlds – our health care informants (Mienczakowski, 1999; Mienczakowski, Smith, & Sinclair, 1996; and Bauman, 1986, cited in Coffey & Atkinson, 1996, p. 76).

To discuss the emotional impacts of ethnodrama performance events we turn first to the play *Syncing Out Loud* (Mienczakowski, 1992/1994), which articulates the lived experiences of patients with mental illness. We have frequently used this example but it is pivotal in explaining the potential ramifications of performed research. In this play an actress-student, who later proclaimed her fundamentalist Christian beliefs, was unintentionally confronted (on stage) by a psychiatric patient suffering from schizophrenia (Morgan, Mienczakowski, & Smith, 2000; Morgan & Mienczakowski, 1999). Harboring undisclosed beliefs that all mentally ill persons, particularly those who share multiple personalities, are possessed by devils, our student actress was understandably horrified when on stage in a live performance at a "secure" psychiatric hospital she found herself confronted by a patient, apparently in psychosis. She believed herself to be speaking directly to the devil. She faltered through her scene, fled the auditorium, and ran out into the night.

Not unpredictably, this incident had serious reverberations for the student, the cast, and the academics and health professionals involved with the performance. At a personal level it forced us to seriously consider the emotional responses and ethical positions of health theater production, and subsequently we came to question the ethical or moral motivations for performing health theater (Mienczakowski, Smith, & Sinclair, 1996, pp. 439–441; Morgan, Mienczakowski, & King, 1999). The ethical and moral desire to constantly reflect upon our actions is thus balanced against substantiation by audience members. For instance, in the following example, insightful data were revealed by someone suffering from a mental illness viewing a performance of the ethnodrama *Syncing Out Loud* (Mienczakowski, 1992/1994):

> As a patient I thought the first scene with the female doctor to be very intense, and very factual. The reasoning behind the audience responding (members of the audience came on stage and argued with the actor/doctor and made speeches to other audience members) was both very therapeutic and

enlightening in some parts. . . . I didn't find it frightening but it did give me a great deal of insight. (*Syncing Out Loud*, 1992/1994)

Again referring to *Syncing Out Loud* (1992/1994), in this instance, the closing scene, "Coming Apart–Coming Together Again" the characters Black 1, 2, and 3 are representations of psychotic thought—personifications of paranoia. Mary, Sean, and Helen are persons with schizophrenia.

COMING APART–COMING TOGETHER AGAIN.

LIGHTS DIM EXCEPT CENTRE STAGE SPOT.

AN ACTOR WALKS INTO THE LIGHT AS THE SPOT IS NARROWED, TO SHOW HER FACE ONLY. A SLOW DRUM BEAT BEGINS. SHE SPEAKS.

Mary : It started very slowly for me. I was alone, ironing, when a gentle voice, inside of me, spoke to me and to me alone. There was no terrifying rush or horrendous confusion.

Black 1: (ENTERING FROM STAGE RIGHT, PARTIALLY OBSCURED BY SHADOWS. WHISPERS) Mary, why do you let them talk to you so?

Mary: Several days went by before anything else happened. Then it was another voice.

Black 2: (ENTERING FROM STAGE LEFT) Hello Mary, I think that you have something important to tell everyone? About why you are here on earth? Go and tell them, Mary. Tell them.

Mary: It was all so gentle. Not at all intimidating. A few weeks later one of the voices told me to—

Black 1: Go to the hospital. When you talk to the doctors, everything will be alright.

Mary: I'd been under tremendous stress. My exams were so important to Mum and Dad. And, I don't know . . . my friends. For months and months I'd been getting the idea that my friends didn't really like me—that they had been talking about me behind my back.

Black 2: Go to the hospital, Mary!

Mary: At the hospital they were very kind, but the voices weren't.

Black 1: You bitch! You are going to pay for this! They are going to pierce your flesh for bringing us here. They will crawl inside your brain and listen and listen to everything you think.

Black 2: We knew it would happen. Save yourself! Run! No. . . . If you stand very still they won't be able to see you. . . .

Mary: So, I stood still whilst my brain was running.
(ALL FREEZE)
Sean: *(ENTERING STAGE RIGHT)* I'd already left home by the time it had started. Dad had kicked me out. Said I was on drugs but I wasn't. He hated me. School was shit, everything I knew was shit. I was shit.
Black 3: *(ENTERING FROM STUDIO FLOOR)* You still here, you little shit?
Sean: Things didn't get any better. I had delusions. I thought that the wardrobe was trying to crush me, to drop on me, at night. I left that place, but *they* came with me.
Black 3: Too right we did. Good for a laugh you were, you little shit.
Mary: I left place after place, because they always caught up with me. I collected smooth round stones because they were special and I made traps for *them* everywhere I went. If I spread talcum powder on the floor of my room, I could tell if they'd been in. I was cleverer than all of them. I had to fight to stop them taking me over. The stones would make ripples in the water and then they wouldn't be able to catch my reflections.
Black 3: But we did, didn't we?
Sean: But they did.
Black 2: Yes, we did.
Sean: *And I was terrified.*
Blacks 1, 2, & 3: Terrified!
Helen: *(ENTERING STAGE LEFT. DRUMPULSE STOPS AS HELEN SPEAKS)* But I'm on medication now and I get a lot of support from my family.
Black 1, 2, & 3: What!?
Helen: And though I know that there are still voices—I don't have to listen to them any more.
Black 1, 2 & 3: Awh! Come off it! What is this?
Mary: I'd been under tremendous stress. My exams were so important to Mum and Dad. And, I don't know, friends.
Black 1: Now that's more like it!
Mary: I left place after place because they always caught up with me. . . .
Sean : So, I stood still whilst my brain was running.
Helen: But I'm on medication now and I get a lot of support from my family.
Sean: And I was terrified. But I'm on medication now and I get a lot of support from my family.
Mary: So I stood still whilst my brain was running.

Sean: I'd been under tremendous stress. My exams were so important to Mum and Dad. And . . . I'm on medication now and I get a lot of support from my family.

(BLACK FIGURES REGISTER THEIR CONCERN THAT THE STATUS QUO IS CHANGING)

Sean & Helen: (HOLDING HANDS) And though I know that there are still voices—I don't have to listen to them any more.

Blacks 2 & 3: Awh, come on! What is this shit?

Black 1: You bitch! you are going to pay for this! They are going to pierce your flesh for bringing us here. But you are on medication now and will get a lot of support from your family. Shit! Who made me say that?

Mary, Sean, & Helen: (ALL HOLDING HANDS—FACING AUDIENCE) And though we know that there are still voices—we don't have to listen to them any more.

All Blacks: Yes, you do! (edited extract, *Syncing Out Loud* (1992/1994) Act II, Scene 7, pp. 69–72.)

As can be seen from this edited extract, in our conception and construction of ethnodrama, we envisioned that it would be a vehicle through which marginalized health care recipients and their caregivers might be given authentic, autonomous public voice. Hence, when deliberating the scene above, my co-researchers and I in close consultation with our corroborating health care informants made a very careful and deliberate choice to end the scene on a positive note for three reasons:

(1) To promote the notion that someone who is "insane" can be "normal" providing he or she is supported, understood, and "keeps taking the tablets"—this message helps to break down the prejudices and superstitions surrounding mental illness. *We wished to explain the perspective of "psychosis" from those experiencing it, at the request of some informants.*

(2) Audiences may also contain persons in the early phase of diagnosis. To stress a pessimistic view, that they are beyond living a relatively normal life, is inaccurate, of no purpose, and could prove intimidating or frightening.

(3) Informants recognized that their best hope resided in medication. As the play also questioned pharmaceutical companies and the "medicine industry" and discussed side-effects, informants felt that the performance should end by declaring to young people that there was also hope.

(4) Our investigations into some of the fallacies surrounding schizophrenia revealed that only 1 in 100,000 persons with schizophrenia in Australia is ever reported as committing a violent act yet a schizophrenia support group we consulted described a pattern of existence and familial disruption of a highly misunderstood and distressing nature.

The ethical route chosen for our script was to support informants and families with messages of hope and insights into how the majority of sufferers experience their worlds. A less biased research approach might have captured a more intimidating and brutal experience of illness than we depicted. But this would have merely been the capturing of particular episodes and incidents rather than the true continuum of lived experience. Someone who suffers from epilepsy, for example, is not well interpreted or understood by the portrayal of an epileptic seizure. We overtly selected our research data to reveal the themes we had documented as positive and "constructive" for families, sufferers, and related professionals. To those who might criticize our framework as a less than purist "constructive" interpretation of research data in relation to positivist notions of perceived "truths," I suggest that they reflect upon the fact that all research is written by people, not by positions or epistemologies. We were explaining the "lived realities" and experiences of certain frequently marginalized health consumers and health professionals.

Emotional Catharsis—Is There Any Other Kind?

Catharsis may, in the context of ethnodrama, be described as a form of "emotional unraveling" for audience members. Indeed, in certain situations, catharsis as emotional unraveling may be a deliberate and desirable goal if one is attempting to empathetically and effectively demonstrate to an audience the lived reality of particular health conditions for clients and health care professionals. Persons relating to the health issue under ethnodrama's scrutiny are likely to attend health theater performances. We have described such audiences as "expert" or "informed" audiences (Morgan & Mienczakowski, 1994; Morgan, Mienczakowski, & King, 1999). They understand in great depth the experiences and conditions being portrayed, either from personal or from professional perspectives. They are well equipped and qualified to contest or contribute to the data presented. Whereas other forms of theater vicariously draw audiences into empathetic emotional relationships, contrastingly, ethnodrama may be frequently seen to reconstruct parallel emotional contexts for its audiences, often drawing upon experiential synergies rather than broad-based human empathies. To this extent the catharsis constructed during ethnodrama performances is more therapeutic than vicariously empathetic. Audience members frequently recall "when this was me," reflecting Geertz's (1988) interpretation of "being there," and thereby are assured that the research performance is cogent. So, performance texts hold the potential to construct "catharsis" for audiences through a collectivization of emotional positions that moves away from empathy (vicarious response) in search of critical emotional (re)action (Mienczakowski, Smith, & Sinclair, 1996).

Emotional Investments in Ethical Performances

To illustrate our concerns about the potentially damaging impact of ethnodrama on vulnerable audients, I present below an abbreviated discussion of a sponsored evaluation of the performance project *Tears in the Shadows* (The Warren Street Theatre Group, 1998),[2] which graphically and unrelentingly explored issues surrounding suicide and sexual assault. From the moment one read the program, one was confronted with the very real consequences of inhabiting data which strongly confronted participants in the process of rehabilitation. To put it more bluntly, the performance was dedicated, by means of the poignant lyrics of a song later thought to be a suicide note, to the memory of a young man who had previously collaborated with the group and who had ended his life under the wheels of a fast-moving train after viewing the play, which included a very graphic suicide scene. The music group's composer hanged himself backstage on the last night of the performance run. It is the very real difficulty of being able to pinpoint the (co)incidence or cross-validation of suicide-related data, as extensively reported by Schmidtke and Haffner (1989), that is of particular concern to me with respect to the ethical responsibilities of those engaged in researching and constructing ethnodrama.

Subsequent to this review, our evaluation team published a set of guidelines (Morgan, Rolfe, & Mienczakowski, 1999) to assist health theater producers incorporate ethical and responsible standards into their ethnodrama. Our intention was, of course, to try to prevent or circumvent the possibility of fostering copycat acts by health care recipients or impeding their recovery progress due to their exposure to a live performance which might be of a questionable or spurious nature. In a close examination of the script and its later performance, we found that the language and imagery of the ethnodrama *Tears in the Shadows* was either ambiguous or so stylized and symbolic as to leave the true meaning or intention obscure—something of real concern to us since we were aware that among the audience were attempted suicides. Further, there were proposals to perform this or similar ethnodramas to very vulnerable and impressionable secondary school students. Similarly, the extremely gothic or bleak overtones of the play featuring explicit suicide and rape scenes provided little by way of positive or uplifting experiences for the audience, and we suggested these scenes' potential to harm vulnerable people, although we would not wish to denigrate or negate the lived experience of the mental health informants who contributed to the construction of the script's text. Indeed, we found that a number of those interviewed post-performance developed closer associations with the themes of suicide and/or sexual assault as a consequence of viewing *Tears in the Shadows*, several of them relating that these reflections were neither positive nor passive in their impact. Somewhat surprisingly a colleague noted that the quite powerful suicide scene and the stylized sexual assault were well received ("enjoyed") by a small percentage of the respondents. Further, a good percentage of the audience believed that the play held an appeal for wider public performance including performance for school age students and many were keen to become involved in post-performance feedback, although this was unable to proceed due to the suicide of a member of the cast.

Immensely disquieting to us, then, is the very real potential of this emotionally carthartic form of dramatic health theater to contribute to a possible relapse or worse still, to a suicide attempt, by those most vulnerable: the health care informants and validating audiences viewing ethnodrama. As previously noted by Morgan, Rolfe, and Mienczakowski (1999), and especially in regards to the use of ethnodrama representing sensitive and abhorrent acts such as suicide and sexual assault to vulnerable school audiences (Kalafat & Elias, 1995; Taylor, 1998), emotive subjects need very careful and measured consideration prior to the development of scripts/texts and public performance. While we would not want to lay the blame for the above-mentioned deaths at the feet of *Tears in the Shadows*, it is considered by the professional reviewers that the performance's forcefulness may have had some potential to contribute to these incidents due to the highly fragile emotional state of persons who were part of the informant health audience. Consequently, we strongly urge producers, directors, and researchers engaging in the ethnodrama process to make good use of the guidelines we (Morgan, Rolfe, & Mienczakowski, 1999) have proposed to minimize the potential risk to vulnerable audiences.

Validatory Analysis

Analysis of audience responses to ethnodramas is one way in which the common values of audience members may be recognized. These responses, analyzed in relation to the informants' control over the script and the production of meanings within ethnodramas, have the potential to assist in the formation of typographies of meanings. If analysis takes place at the public level (in forum settings) the power of meanings generated and collectivized through audience debate can remain within the control of informants and be sustained at a public level. Thus ethnodrama enacts public voice (as opposed to becoming hybridized by the academy) and synergies between agreed meanings may be shared with other audiences and groups also operating at an open, public level.

Validatory Previews

To ensure that performances are actually in a public voice, one which is recognizable and acceptable to informants, it is essential that the representations and meanings generated by an ethnodrama are also recognized and understood by other informants and professionals within the health paradigm being explored. To that end, validatory previews of ethnodramas have typically involved informant groups, representatives of health agencies, and, above all, health consumers who have not been involved in the initial research. During the *Syncing Out Loud* project, persons with schizophrenia and their caregivers (from a day-care health center not otherwise involved in the research) were bussed to the theater in order to assist in validating the play. In the play entitled *Busting: The Challenge of the Drought Spirit* (Mienczakowski & Morgan, 1993), members of a detox center similar to the one represented in the play came to a closed preview. These previews were "closed" to other audiences both in order to protect the identities of audience informants and to guarantee that the discourse was at the level of expert informant understanding.

Theoretical Positioning

Ethnodrama's significance is that it offers theoretical starting points for exploring what we believe to be a relatively under-theorized, barely researched area. It is our contention that the tensions between critical theory, postmodernisms, including feminisms, and the concepts of citizenship and multiculturalism arise from singularities, but that consistent and coherent with these singularities are derivable social tendencies beyond the aggregation of individuality, gender, and ethnicity. This paradoxical social terrain, preliminarily alluded to by some feminist and postcolonial theorists, is that of emotion, desire, religiosity, and the relationships between these (Smith, in Smith & Wexler, 1995; Sinclair, 1995; Mienczakowski, Smith, & Sinclair, 1996).

This feature of the construct of ethnodrama text more closely resembles the ways in which we recognize the patterns and structures that confront us in our everyday existences. We know that understanding of others cannot be demonstrated in one action or event but is dependent upon revelations and responses to multiple situations, each of which contributes to our understanding of overall behavior. So, to portray the multiplicity of lived experience, which is interactive, movable, and contextual in its location, blended composites of verbatim data are constructed to arrive at a characterization of the behaviors and thoughts of a personification of a pathogen. The road traffic accident victim (Olivia) and the psychologist from our current project, *40% Proof* 3 (Mienczakowski & Morgan, 2001, pp. 1–5), dealing with legal processes and recovery, is such a composite example:

Wheelchair/chair center stage. Girl called from audience—she is then seated, bandaged and in obvious discomfort. Various tubes and plastic bags are taped to her body—colostomy, in-tubation incontinence. The medico dressing her with bandages speaks this commentary:

Psychologist: So Olivia, here you are. Can you hear me? Do you remember anything about what has happened to you?
Don't answer—just nod your head—it'll be less painful.
You were in a car. It crashed. You were hurt. Badly hurt. Do you remember anything at all about the accident? *(Olivia shakes her head.)*
You took a ride home—in a car driven by a friend of your girlfriend. The driver was known to you. He'd been drinking. Do you remember that? He hit some traffic lights—doing 120 in a 60 zone. You'd put both feet on the dash prior to impact. You'd obviously prepared yourself for the collision. Feet and arms braced, you must have seen it coming? You were told that you were screaming for him to slow down but he didn't. Do you remember that? The front of the car crumpled as it hit a light pole. Both of your legs were pushed through your pelvis into your thorax. Your pelvis was shattered. Your spleen has been removed. You've lost a finger and your left shoulder was crushed. Your C7 vertebra was broken and your spinal cord bruised. You have brain damage—probably caused when the passenger door caved in on you. It took hours to cut you out of the wreckage. A bystander saved your life—pressing an open artery clotted. You told him you were dying—he said he wouldn't let you. Do you remember?
(She nods.)

Olivia, there are a few things I need to remind you of:
You will probably never walk unaided again.
You have been unconscious for over a month and have little memory of what happened to you.
Your bladder is shot—you'll be incontinent forever and will never be able to go to the bathroom unaided.
You will probably not be able to bear children.
Your vision is now impaired as you seem to have residual brain damage and you will suffer endless infections in your bladder and bowel. Surgery to your groin was extensive.
Your mother will look after you from now on. She'll need to take you home. You will always need care. She has given up her job to look after you.
You will be 26 in November and although your injuries were massive you should live to a ripe old age, providing you stay clear of nasty infections.

On the positive side, your surgery scars have healed really well and will probably disappear almost completely in time. Oh, and your driver friend was almost uninjured but he was found to have a blood alcohol level 3 times higher than the legal limit and so he will probably lose his license.
Olivia: You are kidding—right? (looks at audience.)
Psychiatrist: Any questions?

(Enter Occupational Therapist [OT]. He stands to the left of Olivia and is looking at his clipboard.)

OT: We have a situation where you are worried about your future, I see . . . because after the motor vehicle collision you have had some injuries, I see. Well, as the representative of the Insurer here, I need to evaluate your situation right now, in order to process this claim as fast as we can. . . .
I'll have to give you an examination. OK?
I just have to test to see how mobile you truly are (or are not as the case may be. . . .) Stand please. *(She does so with tremendous effort.)*

(Without warning moves to Olivia and pulls her neck. Olivia jolts and is in pain.)

OT: Yes, I see. . . . *(pulls arm) (Olivia nearly falls and is in more pain.)*
Good reflexes I see. . . . *(pushes her forward)*
(Olivia wobbles, limps and is tearful.)
OT: Hmmm. . . . Mobilising much better. Very good.
Well, I have reviewed the reports on you *(enormous wads of paper evident).* I just need to check a few things now. Please raise your right arm, as high as you can. . . . *(Olivia raises arm to shoulder height.)*
It says you can't get it any higher without agonising pain—But I do need you to try. . . . *(Olivia tries, but in pain.)*
If we know what you can't do, then we can arrange the necessary help. . . . *(Olivia struggles.)*
OT: Good, a pass there then. . . . *(Olivia is very upset.)*
Now then, you were a schoolteacher I see. Well, it seems that you can't stand for long, lift heavy objects or do hard work eh?

> We can put you down for a work trial as a car park attendant then, or as a Professor of the Arts . . . just a joke. . . . *(Olivia looks horrified.)*
> Now its also says that you can't bend over to use the toilet, or get off the toilet unaided, so you piss in a bucket instead. . . . Come along. We'd better see that then, hadn't we? (He produces a bucket.) *(Olivia looks horrified once more.)*
> Well, if not now then later. The psychologist's report notes that you have been distressed and have been crying a lot and feel lonely and isolated and pessimistic about the future. *(Olivia holds head in hands.)*

Thus while we provided our audiences with multiple explanations to examine issues using techniques of contrast and comparison similar to the devices that one experiences with literary texts, a full explanation of the comparisons remained the responsibility of an audience. Whereas in academic texts, writers attempt to frame and produce a logical conclusion to their arguments in order to give meaning, within ethnodramas conclusions are drawn by audiences during performances and are tested in post-performance forum sessions.

Reasonable Responsibilities

In a decade of work we have taken great care to avoid or limit negative outcomes for our informants and audiences. Counsellors and health promotion agencies have always been on hand to offer support to audients during performances. The capacity to offer "debriefing" has remained an integral and valued component of our work. Similarly, learning from the problems encountered by others has also been important. During a performance of Jeanne Mazure's *I'll Give You all the Diamonds in My Teeth* (1993), we remember well the outrage of mental health consumers and their caregivers in the audience who saw mental health consumption dramatized and stereotyped in order to make the performance more "theatrical." While the director defended his interpretation as "theatre and artistry," the audience preferred a more accurate and constructive representation. Their claim was that misrepresentation of health issues was damaging and harmful to audients. We may well ponder upon the real potential for theater to turn litigious where research-based claims and their representations are concerned.

At this point in time David Brown's 1999 *Keep Everything You Love*, an ethnodrama piece by an award-winning Queensland author about at-risk youth and suicide, is no longer financially supported by state health agencies or schools as an earlier version did not comply with the guidelines constructed in 1999. This is a consequence of funding being given to construct a "drama" with good intentions but possibly inadequate professional insight into health-related issues. I am sure it is a good performance piece, but targeting school-age students with theater using suicide ideation as a vehicle seems to be interpreted by health agencies and concerned educators as undesirable. Formerly called, *Kill Everything You Loved*, the play has undergone some changes to address earlier concerns relating to efficacy. While never dreaming of stifling creative work we are very concerned about protecting at-risk school age groups.

Certainly our work reviewing other performance groups in suicide prevention has given us cause for concern. Consequently, we would strongly urge that producers, directors, and researchers engaging in the ethnodrama process take care to minimize the potential risk to vulnerable audiences (Morgan, Rolfe, & Mienczakowski, 1999). Not for a moment, though, do we propose that these warnings should prevent the continuation of our work. They serve only to deepen the connection between performance, research, and productive outcomes. The construction of a new aesthetic through which such performance work can be interpreted and experienced is an urgent step toward providing a framework to guide this emergent trend of performed research data.

Notes

1. Performance in a residential psychiatric unit.
2. For a more thorough report of this, see Morgan, Mienczakowski, & Smith, 2000, pp. 172–176.
3. These edited data are drawn from an exploration of the experiences of road traffic accident victims and the perusal of compensation claims through legal processes. Working with a professional psychologist frequently paid by legal services and/or insurance companies to assess psychological impacts realted to recovery processes, this excerpt examines the roles of medical professionals and insurance representatives in compensation claims.

References

Bauman, Zygmunt. (1986). *Hidden economy: East and West.* Washington, D.C.: National Council for Soviet and East European Research.

Bauman, Zygmunt. (1992). *Intimations of postmodernity.* London: Routledge.

Bauman, Zygmunt. (2000). *Liquid modernity.* Malden, MA: Blackwell.

Blumer, H. (1976). The methodological position of symbolic interactionism. In M. Hammersley & P. Woods (Eds.), The process of schooling. London: Routledge & Kegan Paul.

Boal, A. (1985). *Theatre of the oppressed.* (C. A. & M. L. McBride, Trans.). New York: Theatre Communications Group. (Original work published 1979)

Brown, D. (1999). *Keep everything you love.* Brisbane: PlayLab.

Coffey, A., & Atkinson, P. (1996). Making sense of qualitative data: Complementary research strategies. Thousand Oaks, CA: Sage.

Courtney, R. (1981). The universal theatre. In G. Schattner & R. Courtney (Eds.), *Drama in therapy.* (Vols. 1 & 2.). New York: Drama Book Specialists.

Geertz, C. (1988). *Works and lives: The anthropologist as an author.* Stanford, CA: Stanford University Press.

Hebdidge, D. (1988). *Hiding in the light: On images and things.* London: Routledge.

Kalafat, J., & Elias, M. (1995). Suicide in an educational context. *Suicide and Life Threatening Behaviors, 1*(25), 123–133.

Mazure, J. (1993). *And I'll give you all the diamonds in my teeth.* Unpublished play, reviewed by J. Edge in *The Bulletin, 115*(5883), 91.

McLaren, P. (1995). *Critical pedagogy and predatory culture: Oppositional politics in a postmodern era.* London: Routledge.

Mienczakowski, J. (1994). *Syncing out loud: A journey into illness* (2nd ed.). Brisbane, Australia: Griffith University Reprographics.

Mienczakowski, J. (1995). The theatre of ethnography: The reconstruction of ethnography into theatre with emancipatory potential. *Qualitative Inquiry, 1*(3), 360–375.

Mienczakowski, J. (1996). An ethnographic act: The construction of consensual theater. In C. Ellis & A. Bochner (Eds.), *Composing ethnography* (pp. 244–266). Thousand Oaks, CA: Altamira Sage.

Mienczakowski, J. (1999). Ethnography in the hands of participants: Tools of dramatic discovery. *Studies in Educational Ethnography,* 2, 145–161. Stamford, CT: JAI Press.

Mienczakowski, J., & Morgan, S. (1993). *Busting: The challenge of the drought spirit.* Brisbane, Australia: Griffith University Reprographics.

Mienczakowski, J., & Morgan, S. (2001). Data extract from "*40% Proof.*" Research in progress.

Mienczakowski, J., Smith, R., & Sinclair, M. (1996). On the road to catharsis: A theoretical framework for change. *Qualitative Inquiry,* 2(4), 439–462.

Morgan, S. (1999). *Tears in the shadows: A performance evaluation.* Unpublished manuscript.

Morgan, S., & Mienczakowski, J. (1993). Re-animation of the research report: Shaping nursing theory and practice. *Monograph 2.* Melbourne, Australia: La Trobe University Press.

Morgan, S., & Mienczakowski, J. (1994). The application of critical ethnodrama to health settings. *Victorian Association of Drama in Education Journal, 16,* 15–19.

Morgan, S., & Mienczakowski, J. (1999, February). *Ethical dilemmas in performance ethnography: Examples from ethnodrama and theatre*. Paper presented at Couch Stone Symposium, SSSI Conference, Las Vegas, NV.

Morgan, S., Mienczakowski, J., & King, G. (1999). *The dramatic representation of suicide: Issues, concerns and guidelines.* (Audiotape recording March 25). Melbourne, Australia: Suicide Prevention Convention Center.

Morgan, S., Mienczakowski, J., & Smith, L. (2000). Extreme dilemmas in performance ethnography: Unleashed emotionality of performance in critical areas of suicide, abuse and madness. In K. Gilbert (Ed.), *Emotional nature of qualitative research*. Boca Raton, FL: CRC Press LLC.

Morgan, S., Rolfe, A., & Mienczakowski, J. (1999). Exploration! Intervention! Education! Health promotion!: A developmental set of guidelines for the presentation of dramatic performances in suicide prevention. In S. Robertson, K. Kellehear, M. Teeson, & V. Miller (Eds.), *Making history, shaping the future: The 1999 mental health services conference*. Rozelle, NSW, Australia: Standard Publishing House.

Schattner, G., & Courtney, R. (Eds.). (1981). *Drama in therapy (*Vols. 1 & 2). New York: Drama Book Specialists.

Schmidtke, A., & Haffner, H. (1989). Public attitudes towards and effects of the mass media on suicidal and self-harm behaviour. In R. F. W. Diekstra and the World Health Organization (Eds.), *Suicide and its prevention*. Leiden, Netherlands: Brill.

Sinclair, M. (1995). *From "B" effect to "C" effect: The rhetoric and practice of aboriginal self-determination.* Unpublished honors thesis, Griffith University, Gold Coast, Queensland, Australia.

Smith, R. (1995). Prologue. In R. Smith & P. Wexler (Eds.), *After postmodernism: Education, politics and identity* (pp.1–9). London: Falmer.

Taylor, B. (1998). *Educating for life: Guidelines for effective suicide prevention programs in secondary schools.* Melbourne, Australia: Taylor Education.

Turner, V. (1986). *The anthropology of performance.* New York: Performing Arts Journal Publications.

Warren Street Theatre Group. (1998). *Tears in the shadows.* Unpublished play.

CHAPTER 4

Staging a Study

Performing the Personal and Professional Struggles of Beginning Teachers

DWIGHT ROGERS, PAUL FRELLICK, AND LESLIE BABINSKI

The first year of teaching is a trying and often traumatic time for beginning teachers. New teachers are frequently thrust into classrooms with little support and few materials. It is one of the few jobs in which novices are asked to do the same work as veterans, with fewer resources and typically under more difficult circumstances. In an attempt to assist these new teachers and understand more about their first-year experiences, we (Leslie and Dwight) organized a total of 19 discussion-based support groups for 100 beginning teachers in the Piedmont region of North Carolina from 1995 to 2000. These new teacher groups consisted of three to nine members and met biweekly. Our goal was to help these beginning teachers address the many pedagogical, organizational, administrative, and personal issues confronting them each day through engaging them in regularly scheduled collaborative problem-solving discussions with their peers.

The group discussions were filled with stories of the hardships and isolation faced by many of these new teachers each school day. Leslie and Dwight's first attempt to capture some of the teachers' experiences was presented in the form of a research report. But we found this process and its final product to be empty, lifeless, and extremely unsatisfying. This report did not evoke the drama or emotion that was present in many of our new teacher meetings. Despite our frequent use of their direct quotes, the teachers' voices seemed muted and inauthentic. The urgency and dramatic nature of the teachers' stories induced us to consider presenting their experiences in a mode of presentation similar to the group discussions. We felt that presenting the teachers' words in the form of a play might convey the intensity of their emotions and concerns in a way that journal articles or academic presentations typically do not. This play, reproduced later in the chapter, is based on the voices of beginning elementary teachers taken from transcripts of new teacher group meetings and exit interviews of 49 elementary teachers who participated in the groups from 1995 to 1998. The stories that make up the basis of our play were recorded as the new teachers were talking to their colleagues in the discussion groups and/or through end-of-the-year interviews focusing on their experiences as novices in the profession.

Playing with the Data: A Brief History of Our Research/Artistic Collaboration

I (Paul) came to the project from my work as a theater director and sometime adaptor of texts to the stage. Dwight and Leslie introduced me to the new teacher group project and showed me some of the stories they'd collected. I was intrigued by the dramatic potential of these transcripts of group discussions and exit interviews, as well as by the challenge of finding a theatrical realization of these analytical and emotional accounts of first-year teaching experiences.

The data, as noted earlier, had been collected and a report published, in accordance with the original intentions of the study. The idea of a dramatic presentation did not shape the data; it grew out of the findings themselves and Dwight and Leslie's dissatisfaction with the inability of their published work to convey the power of the data. Unlike the dramatizing of an extant study that Paget (1990) documents, we began to envision this new presentation as a parallel but wholly different expression of the data, and our process became an exploration of the capabilities of our chosen medium to accomplish that expression.

Our first draft of the play was an experiment in this new mode of data presentation. Our original draft was based on the experiences of three teachers in one of our groups and was more like a collage of stories to be performed than like a play. Leslie, Dwight, and two other colleagues performed the original play as readers' theater for the three teachers whose lives were portrayed in the presentation. We found that presenting the teachers' voices as a play and "feeding back" their lives/our data to them made possible new and unexpected critical space.

"Feeding back the data" in the form of a play is an attempt to make "data" about the experiences of beginning teachers more accessible to teachers and administrators while also making more visible and visceral the conditions under which some teachers live their professional lives. We wanted to re-present the intensity of the emotional reactions of the teachers' voices and to let the teachers "talk for themselves" by using their own words. Unexpectedly, the "feeding back" of data in the form of a play began the process of opening up critical space which seemed to give the beginning teachers an opportunity to reclaim self-worth by hearing their struggles. We agreed that a dramatic presentation of this data would provide an excellent catalyst for discussion of the problems identified by the first-year teachers, one that might even instigate action toward solving some of those problems.

Our intention, ultimately, was to re-create, in the presentation of data, the drama and emotion that had characterized the data collection process. As Brustein (1987) points out, the advantage the theater has over other media is its "immediacy," as opposed to the "remote, aloof, involuntarily engaged" nature of the audience of films, television, narrative fiction, and, one might add, research reports. He goes on to note that, while we prefer to watch movies alone or in small groups, "theatre-going is a communal act . . . one of a dwindling group of activities that bring Americans into communication with each other." That communication was precisely what we were hoping to engender.

Leslie and Dwight had already identified themes within the data, denoting common threads among the participants' statements and responses. This categorization had been done as part of preparing the initial research report, but it was crucial to the playwriting process as well. It enabled us to group passages around certain concerns, and subsequently select examples from the data that would reflect both the specificity and the diversity of the data. We wanted to make sure that all six of the themes we identified in our analysis were represented in the play.

Through the utilization of these themes, many similar stories emerged, and we began selecting those stories that most effectively embodied a given theme. We looked for stories that featured conflict, action, humor, pathos, and other qualities that would engage the audience members. Many of the first-year teachers, for example, spoke of the process that had brought them to teaching, but we selected the story of one teacher who found herself in the middle of her first "teachable moment" accidentally, in the midst of encouraging a child's desire to become a farmer. That story displayed the passion that many of the other teachers mentioned in a simple, straightforward fashion, developing out of the dramatic situation of a child rescued from humiliation. Even more important, the story *illustrates* the speaker's feelings, rather than merely noting or listing them.

That preference toward illustration was central to our choice of theatrical presentation for the data. We did not set out to prove something as much as to "re-present" the data that had been "presented" to us. We knew the data provided plenty of answers to the fundamental research question of "What is going on here?" but they also raised a number of questions—questions that could lead to a fuller understanding of the first-year teaching experience as a whole or to ideas and actions to improve that experience. We wanted our audience to ask those questions.

Consequently, we eschewed any narration or explanatory passages, relying entirely on the actual words of the participants to convey the information included in our data. From the beginning, we wanted our presentation to instigate further discussion, and we were determined not to preclude that discussion by reaching and then presenting our own conclusions.

Certain practical considerations also shaped the process. Given our desire to include discussion as a necessary component of the presentation, we opted to limit the play to about 15 minutes. We also needed to limit the presenters—our data came from a large number of teachers, and we didn't want to diffuse the presentation by having too many actors (let alone trying to assemble them for rehearsal and performance).

We decided on a cast of four or five, but this led to other questions: Would each actor present only one teacher's comments? Would each actor portray a set of teachers and change voice or costume to indicate which "character" he or she was presenting? Or would we try to somehow spread the different voices among the cast?

Here we were guided in part by the responses of the subjects of the original trial presentation. In that instance, the teachers were profoundly impacted by hearing their own stories, but the intimacy of that event was very different from the events we envisioned, and that audience was very different from the audiences we would try to reach in the future. We realized that we would need to use a more diverse set of voices in order to speak to a more diverse audience. Simply presenting the experiences of three individuals would be less likely to reflect the experiences or to address the prejudices of a large audience.

We also wanted to avoid spending time identifying voices (e.g., having actors speak an individual's name before each speech), and in order to make our final text useful to a wide variety of groups, we wanted to create a presentation that was not dependent on "acting skills" to convey a clear sense of which individual was speaking (e.g., changing vocal patterns). Ultimately, we chose to present a "chorus" of voices, whose testimony to a variety of experiences would create a fuller portrait of the first year of teaching. In any case, the data were better suited to this method of portrayal, given that we did not have much biographical information on the individuals involved.

We decided to distribute our data between four voices, labeling them with letters only, and made no effort to create specific characters, leaving the audience to make their own suppositions as they wished. We assigned stories and dialogue in such a way that no character seemed to behave in a contradictory fashion (e.g., expressing satisfaction with the work environment in one scene and complaining about it in another) and removed specific information that might prove confusing (e.g., grade levels that would differ from story to story). The effect was to focus the piece on the aggregate data rather than on the individual sources.

As data were selected for presentation, a structure began to emerge. Inherent in much of the data was a straightforwardness resulting from how the data were solicited. Many of the passages we selected were instances of the participants communicating their experiences and responses in answer to specific questions. We wanted to preserve the simple directness of those expressions and determined that such data should be communicated directly to the audience as they had been originally to the interviewer. Other data were originally the result of a group dynamic, and consequently we attempted to maintain that dynamic in the presentation, allowing the characters to share stories conversationally. Always our intention was to present not only the data but also the honesty and power that had been a part of their initial presentation (i.e., at collection).

We then shaped the play as a playwright would, looking to create a piece with a beginning, middle, and end, a piece that would grow in intensity and build to a climax that could provoke intellectual and emotional responses in the audience. This shaping involved selecting passages that conveyed certain information or a certain mood, that built upon or provided a contrast to a previously selected passage, or that had a certain length or rhythm appropriate to a particular section of the piece. We did some editing as well, to convey the participants' intent more succinctly or to connect more easily to an adjoining passage.

This was a necessary part of the process, but we entered into it cautiously, concerned that in our desire for dramatic impact we might alter the data for our own purposes. We were committed to using only the words in the transcripts, but even the editing of those words could change the sense of a passage from the original speaker's intent. One such passage, later removed, involved a story about a mentor who was "micro-managing" the first-year teacher. The story was a good example of how a system designed to help the teacher was actually hindering her—a common thread throughout our data—and the narrative effectively conveyed the mentor's invasiveness and the new teacher's growing discomfort. But the teacher went on to assert that eventually she had come to see the mentor's actions as beneficial, effectively blunting the impact of her story. We considered using only the first part of the story—certainly the facts and experiences were valid and evocative. Yet we felt that by excluding part of the story, we were telling a different one than the teacher's, and consequently failing in our attempt to present our data honestly.

Our determination to maintain fidelity to the data checked any inclination to use the data to suit a particular purpose. We knew we could not craft the play (or a report, for that matter) without operating according to certain biases, but by insisting that the selected passages remain in the speaker's words and reflect the speaker's intent, we significantly limited our ability to make propaganda of our data.

As the play took shape, we worked to reinforce the theatricality of the stories told, in order to engage the audience more fully. When characters other than the storyteller emerged in the data, for example, we determined that the other actors on stage would take on those parts. We decided to approach this play-acting in a slightly more presentational manner than the realistic one employed otherwise; this choice again eliminated the need for subtle acting skills, and at the same time helped to heighten the presence of the characters conjured by the storyteller. The staging we employed was simple, intended primarily to keep the audience aware that the classroom was at the center of all of the experiences related. A table and four chairs helped create that environment, and the actors moved through them as they would in a classroom.

We arrived at a piece whose structure seemed effective but whose length was excessive, and so we began to winnow the data further. We elected not to include some passages because, out of the context of the original interview or discussion, their import or focus became significantly different. Other passages presented valid perspectives, but simply didn't fit the developed structure or seemed less important to the whole than other passages.

The final stage of the development process was to present the piece to sample audiences of new teacher group facilitators (i.e., audiences privy to similar data, in effect cross-checking and validating our data). We asked them about their impressions of the piece and noted the impact certain passages had on them.

The placement of certain speeches proved to be an important issue, particularly since we were attempting to craft a portrait of the experience that reflected the variety of perspectives included in our data. The difference between ending the piece on its most strident note ("there's like no light at the end of this tunnel") and concluding with the more ambiguous plaint ("Before I started teaching, I thought I would want to teach forever") was considerable when played before an audience; even though both passages were included, ending with the former passage seemed to give additional weight to its bleakness beyond the support of the data.

This process led to the script reproduced on the next page. We have included it not only as a reference for the reader of this chapter but also in the hope that it will be performed by others interested in the conditions faced by first-year teachers. "Of Trailers and Trenches" had its premiere at the AERA conference in Montreal, Canada, in spring 1999.

OF TRAILERS AND TRENCHES

(School bell rings. Children's voices are heard loudly, as if moving through the hall, then subside. Lights reveal four teachers, standing and facing the audience. There is a table stage left with two rows of chairs facing it.)

A: I decided to become a teacher, well, I think when I was born. I don't know. I just think it was just that whole mentality growing up, because my mom taught in the school system, and I spent pretty much my life there, you know. So I think a lot of it is based on the fact that I was raised in the school.

B: At the end of freshman year, I went home to visit a teacher that I had, and I got a chance to speak to all of the classes. They had questions about college and stuff. There was a little kid who raised his hand and wanted to know where he could go to college to be a farmer. The class just busted out laughing over it. It was awful. I think that was the first teachable moment I had, because I was like "How many people here eat?" And they all raised their hand. I said, "If there is not somebody like that out there when you get older, you won't. You know what, with the way you need to increase crop yields and the way you have to mix fertilizers and chemicals and this, that and the other, you better hope that this person wants to go to college to figure these things out so you don't eat something and croak over dead."

C: I've always loved kids ever since I can remember. I started baby-sitting when I was little and my parents had foster children that I loved to take care of. I wanted to have my own kids until I started teaching.

D: I expected my teaching experience to be like my student teaching. I expected school spirit. I expected respect from the children. I expected support from other teachers. A sense of belonging. I knew I wasn't going to have a perfect year but I really thought I was prepared to be a teacher. I didn't know diddly-squat.

A: In order to teach these children, I have to think like these children. I have to act like them sometimes, too, in order to get their attention. Which I have done pretty well. I can act like a six-year-old.

C: A good teacher should be able to take a reasonable

range of kids, from high ability to not so great ability, and create activities and lessons that will meet those needs. Activities that everybody can do, without saying, "*You* are not that bright, you need to work on reading skills. *You're* bright, you can do fun and cool projects all day long."

B: I have one child that I put my phone number on the top of his homework sheet every day because he wants to make sure he can . . . he doesn't call me, but it's the comfort of knowing it is there if he needs me.

C: (sitting, speaking to the other teachers): I student-taught ten weeks with first grade and six weeks with kindergarten. I just did fun things. We learned some Japanese writing. I went to a restaurant and had them write down the children's names in Japanese and I was so motivated. I am not motivated to do that now because I have so many other things to do. It is not that I don't have time because I think I am one of those people that I'll *make* time to do it. But I am so exhausted, so tired, so bogged down by everything that I have to do.

B: (likewise sitting and addressing other teachers): I started teaching first grade on December 16 th or something like that. It was the week before Christmas break.

I thought that the woman before me was retiring at the end of December. So I called to confirm that I would come Monday to do observations and to kind of get to know the kids for that whole week. They said they had me down to start *working*.

That Monday. So that was kind of hairy.

D: *(likewise sitting and addressing other teachers):* My program, it didn't prepare us for the things that can't be prepared for. Julie's Mom dying around October. Lauren on the playground pissing in her pants. You are put in a position—it is not like we practiced that. Dealing with the parents. That is just you. And until you are put in that position you don't know what you are going to do. The bureaucratic crap that happens and stuff like that. You really have to get out there in the trenches and find out for yourself.

A: (sitting and joining the others): This is kind of personal, but my jaw—I guess it was around Thanksgiving that it started hurting and I was clenching my teeth and it hurt to open it and it would pop and I went to the dentist and he said it was because of stress and I was going to have to get a $300 mouthpiece.

C: I was ready to quit twelve days after school started.

(School bell rings. Children's voices are heard again, then subside. Teacher D rises as she talks to the other teachers.)

D: I started recorded books with some of my low readers. And it's been a huge success. I go home and tape the books. Then I set up listening centers and they listen to the books three times. They have to track the words and then read it back to me within 30 minutes. And that just puts it in their short-term memory. But it is such a confidence builder because, for the first time in their life, they're actually reading.

C: That's great.

D: But it's just hard right now to try to work out the kinks of managing six or eight children. You know, like a system, because we only have two tape recorders. Trying to keep it going while keeping the rest of them on track, you know. And my assistant just had her baby yesterday.

B: Could you keep it going if you had more tape recorders?

D: Yeah, it's a huge problem.

C: You might check the PTA Thrift Shop.

D: That's not the point! We shouldn't have to do that!

A: They expect us to teach all these things, but they don't provide us with the things to teach it. *(Teacher D sits.)*

B: Like I don't feel I have gotten any support from the administration or other teachers. My first week here I didn't have anything except a trailer and 30 desks. No supplies, nothing on the walls, I didn't even have any bookcases. I was a wreck. I would go home thinking, "Oh my god, I can't do this, I can't do this!" Because I didn't feel like I could turn to anyone. Even though there were all these other first year teachers, they were in the same boat I was. We were all putting our arms up in the air thinking, "I don't know what to do! We don't know what to do!"

A: (rising and addressing the group): A quarter of my class . . . they are not happy children. I don't know. But I felt like they came into this room and they just really, really needed more than just to know the counties of

North Carolina. There are some kids who don't need that. They don't need me at all, really. But these kids did and I wasn't expecting that. I wasn't expecting to be so important. (Teacher *C* sits on table.)

C: (rising and addressing the group): José came in at the beginning of the year and was just a pistol, I mean his attitude was so bad and he was the one I was always griping about. José this and José that. Why can't he just do his work? You know,

ALL:
Yada yada yada.

C: And finally, I had made so much progress with him and he was writing these things. I mean I copied almost all of his writing samples because of the language he used. He's an ESL student and he was using all this vocabulary that was just outrageous. He's just a sensational writer. And he warmed up to me, I guess, because he just started doing his work and I just made so much progress. And then the principal came in.

A: (as principal): Um, José's family is moving. Today is his last day.

C: Today?

A: (as principal): (nods) Can you tell him?

D: Just leave it to the teacher to deliver the bad news.

C: So what I did was I took him outside and sat him down and just told him that today was his last day, and he just, he got so sad. And it was a Friday and for the afternoon we were having a program. And I said, "Do you want to spend the afternoon with me?" And he said yeah. *(sits on table next to Teacher B)* So I had my assistant take the class down to the program, and he came back to the classroom with me and read books to me. And we just talked and I gave him treats and going away presents and stuff like that. I just feel like . . . I didn't want him to leave. He was my, my student, you know. I feel like I made so much progress with him, and now he's going to a new school with a new teacher. . . . *(Teacher B goes and sits down with the others.)*

And we all wrote him letters and he wrote us a letter. *(Teacher C opens a folded piece of paper, reads it to herself. Then, to others:)* He said he was sad 'cause he missed all his friends. And he said his class was doing division, and he didn't know how to do it. *(Teacher C refolds the letter.)* And I thought,

"Division? I'm way behind."

(Teacher C returns to chair. All four teachers turn their chairs into a semicircle.)

A: When I look back at what my students were reading at the beginning of the year and what they can read now and I think, "Wow, they have come a long way." It has been hard for me to see it as we go along. I looked at some of the journals from the first day of school. . . .

B: You really did teach them something!

A: Yeah! Sometimes it amazes me to think that because you have these days where you feel like you haven't taught them anything.

D: I don't know, I'm a little overwhelmed with everything, you know. I mean, it's almost April, we're going into Spring break, we only have eight weeks left. I feel like I'm behind. And I walk in in the morning and I'm like, I don't have anything good planned for today. This is going to be a bad day. You know, and I mean you run out of ideas, literally.

C: I started going through this phase a couple of weeks ago as to whether I would be teaching next year.

A: Really?

C: I thought I would move up to Alaska and work with the bus service—that's what always seems appealing on rough days.

B: My special needs students are like a hurricane in my room. They are laughing, they are squealing, and they're throwing each other, wrestling on the ground and slamming into each other.

D: Oh, man.

B: But they're just so big and so heavy and we have to wear weight lifting belts all day long. Cause they won't—if we hurt ourselves handling the kids without wearing the belt they will not pay workman's comp.

A: God, I can't believe it.

B: So we have to wear these friggin' belts all day.

D: They're not belts, they're like a vest.

B: It's like a corset.

A: It's like what the UPS drivers wear, right? I can't believe it.

B: And physically I'm just exhausted at the end of every day because there's so much physical handling.

A: It's like if you don't know how to drive a forklift, you can't get your teaching certification.

D: This school has really gotten to me. I've turned into a monster. I mean, I hear some of the things I say to my children and I'm like, "What?" I made a child eat in the corner of the room today, on the floor. Eat his lunch. I was just like, "Don't look at me! Don't talk to me! I don't want to see you!" I left him in there. I mean, this is something I would not do.

C: I catch myself yelling at my kids too.

A: I do too, and I don't like it.

C: And it's like man, what did I just do to them?

D: Yeah, and it also carries over into all aspects of your life. I feel like my patience for people has declined. Like, I'm not even talking about my kids who drive me crazy, absolutely crazy. But I feel like I'm also more short with my parents, my boyfriend, my friends. I'm just like, I'm not happy. I'm not the same person I was when I graduated from college in May. You know, and I'm not the same person I was in August when I got hired.

B: But you wouldn't be the same person even if—

D: No, but I *liked* that person! I don't like me now. I liked who I was. I mean not the person, but the type of person I was. My whole personality was different. I mean, I would never, you know. . . . If I had been a fly on the wall and heard some of the things that I say to my students, oh my god! It's just not, it's not what I want to be.

(Bell rings again. The children's voices follow, then fade to the sound of echoing footsteps under the following. The teachers stand as at the beginning of the play facing out and addressing the audience.)

A: I never expected to be in a situation like this. I never expected to feel so down and so incompetent. I think a lot of it didn't have to happen. A lot of my grief and uncertainties about myself and about me as a teacher and my profession, I just don't think it was necessary. I mean, I have always been a go-getter. But there have been times where I felt so small that I couldn't even scrape myself off of the floor.

D: Yeah well, teaching this year has definitely taken my dreams and flushed them down the toilet. I don't feel like

I'm going anywhere with this profession. I mean, there's like no light at the end of this tunnel.

B: I really did fall in love with the kids and the whole profession and I didn't expect that. I expected it to be a lot of work and it was. It is. The volume of what they want you to put down on paper is kind of amazing to me. But then again, I've talked with people at other school systems and they seem to have more than I do. People who can't go home in the afternoons until their lesson plans are laid on their desk and the principal comes by and checks.

C: I'm so tired from this year. I wouldn't want to put any less into it, into these children. It is just going to tire me out. I think I will do it for five years or a little bit more, but unless something happens. . . .

Before I started teaching, I thought I would want to teach forever.

(Lights fade. Bell rings again in darkness.)

END OF PLAY

Reflections

Directing a play and adapting a work for the stage can both be reduced to the same basic task: to frame or shape a story or event in order to maximize its impact on an audience. The director takes a script, determines its central themes and events, and shapes the production to emphasize those elements; the adaptor takes a text or texts (e.g., a novel or a set of historical accounts) and selects the elements that are absolutely necessary to tell the story on stage. In the course of working on "Of Trailers and Trenches," we discovered—much as Donmoyer and Yennie-Donmoyer (1995) did, that the "processes of data analysis and . . . script construction were really not much different" (p. 9). Dwight and Leslie had identified central themes in the data and extracted significant examples to illustrate their findings. The task of selecting and presenting data through a play was, then, a natural extension of the research process and Paul's previous work in the theater.

Like Donmoyer and Yennie-Donmoyer, we struggled with the role aesthetic judgment plays in creating a dramatic representation of data. Precisely because such judgments are sometimes difficult to articulate beyond the assertion that the result "feels right," defending each of the vast number of choices that go into each page of each draft (e.g., placement of speeches, retention of grammatical errors) is a largely pointless exercise. An artist's instincts are often his chief resource, one he is better off exploring than justifying.

The theater, however, is a collaborative art form, and so we dealt with this dilemma in a collaborative manner. By soliciting feedback from the data collectors and others familiar with the issues at hand, we were able to lessen the likelihood that our choices would misrepresent the data. The process is not risk-free, but then, any presentation of data is vulnerable to misinterpretation by a reader. Our task was not to find a representation free of ambiguity but to highlight the power of the data without exacerbating that ambiguity.

The scientific regimen is a standard not usually imposed on a theatrical work. The creation of composite characters or the manipulation of facts is generally understood as necessary when crafting a film or play about actual figures and events; even documentary films are often called to task for taking such liberties as altering the chronology of events. No one expects a chronicler to be able to tell the story of a yearlong event comprehensively in the course of two hours.

Of course, any time that a sampling of information is allowed to stand for a much larger set of data, aspects of that larger set will be lost. The task that filmmakers, playwrights, and other storytellers face, however, is to create a compelling account that can engage an audience, to give expression to truths within the story that may transcend the "facts" of the case. There are surely many stories to be told that would reflect the data Dwight and Leslie collected, stories that would be true to the sentiments expressed if not to the particulars of the data.

But our suspicion that the actual words of first-year teachers discussing their experiences would have an impact that needed no dramatic elaboration has proven to be true. While performances of the play have elicited a variety of responses, audiences have frequently noted the vividness of the data, easily recalling specific passages and identifying with a particular speaker. Even some of the performers have mentioned the impact certain speeches have had on them.

There remain a number of limitations to presenting our data in the form of a play. We greatly limit the size of the audience by presenting the new teachers' stories as a play, and there are considerable logistical, organizational, personnel, and resource problems to deal with each time we stage the play. The audience, unlike the reader of a journal article, cannot return to the data at will. And although we strongly believe that the play allows us to hear the teachers' voices more fully and with more resonance, we have some concern that presenting the data in an unmediated fashion, with no interpretation or guidance from the researchers, may lead to misinterpretation.

Each performance carries with it a possibility of disappointment—a performance that fails to convey certain information or feeling, a discussion that fails to address the concerns contained in the data, and so on. However, unlike rereading a research article or report, we have found that even after many performances of our play, we do not get tired of performing or watching others perform the script. Like teaching at its best, each performance seems fresh and new. It is generative, and its immediacy thus encourages further reflection and examination of the issues faced by new teachers.

Because of its ability to evoke feelings and stimulate discussion, we believe our play may provide a powerful way to encourage veteran and novice teachers alike to share their stories to help us gain a deeper understanding of their lived experiences as beginning teachers. The comments we have received from teachers who have seen our play suggest that it may provide a more powerful and evocative stimulus for encouraging individuals to talk frankly and openly about their teaching than a typical interview situation.

To date, we have not performed "Of Trailers and Trenches" in any fashion other than as a staged reading (i.e., the actors reading from scripts and performing with only minimal staging, without the benefit of lights, costumes, or other production elements). Nevertheless, the piece has reaffirmed for us the power of the theater at its most basic—human beings brought into concert by story. Despite the limitations and even dangers of a dramatic presentation of data (e.g., omission, confusion, misinterpretation, and many others), the power inherent in the very human connection that the theater forges seems to us a wonderful tool for researchers. And reciprocally, research, like the new teacher study that led to this play, can be an important resource for dramatists.

References

Brustein, R. (1987). *Who needs theatre: Dramatic opinions.* New York: Atlantic Monthly Press.

Donmoyer, R., & Yennie-Donmoyer, J. (1995, April) *Data as drama: Reflections of the use of readers' theater as an artistic mode of data display.* Paper presented at the Annual Meeting of the American Educational Research Association, San Francisco.

Paget, M. A. (1990). Performing the text. *Journal of Contemporary Ethnography, 19*(1), 136–155.

PART TWO

Music and Poetry Data

CHAPTER 5

Sweeping the Temple: A Performance Collage

TERRY JENOURE

Dear Patti,
It's been much too long since we last saw each other, but I think about you all the time now. I have the feeling you may be able to give me some guidance and so I'm writing to find out how you feel about the idea of turning my research into a performance. You've always trusted me and gotten excited about our work, but I thought it might be best to check with you anyway. I look forward to hearing from you.
Always with love,
Terry

From Patti to the Portrait

In 1993 Patti was my best friend. We had known each other for nearly 20 years and probably the strongest connection between us was our performing. Patti danced and I made music. We did this together year after year. We made performances for concerts and we made them in our living rooms. But we always made them for us/for fun. The best thing about our collaborations was the energy and enthusiasm for work/play that we brought to them.

Then, one evening Patti called me. It was late. I was startled. I was sitting on my bed. I remember how cold and hard the phone felt against my face and how still my room seemed as she told me in her clipped, matter-of-fact way that she had breast cancer. Unusually calm, she appeared upset only because she had just begun a college teaching job a year earlier and would now have to take a leave of absence. Like her, I forced myself not to feel too much, and during the two years or so that she battled the cancer, I always tried to match my emotions with hers.

At some point during her medical treatment I began doing research for a project that was later to become a book (Jenoure, 2000). I was looking to interview African American musicians, dancers, and visual artists who teach in colleges and universities that have traditionally been White institutions. Given that African American artists are represented in very low numbers in higher education, I was hoping to find out about some of their experiences at schools, why and how they did their work, and what meaning they made of it (Seidman, 1991). Interviewing 12 people, I wanted to get as balanced a group as possible in terms of their gender, art forms, ages, and degrees of teaching experience, and I thought Patti would fit nicely into this mix.

> [sung]
> *I don't remember saying I'm Negro*
> *I don't remember saying I'm Colored*
> *I don't remember saying I'm Black*

I considered the possibility that interviewing her might be a conflict of interest. But I wanted to include her in the study and decided that, given the state of her health and her excitement about my work, the only thing that really mattered was our having this chance to share something very special. I think we both wondered if it might be our last collaboration. So, over the next couple of months Patti and I talked, arranging our meetings around her chemotherapy and its devastating physical and emotional effects. I interviewed her at my home and hers. In spite of our friendship and the intensity of the conditions, I tried my best to treat her as I did the other participants, an effort that now seems so odd and futile—so sad. I was embarrassed when many of her stories about how she developed as an artist involved me. Here I was, trying to maintain a respectable amount of scholarly distance, and to conduct myself as formally and impartially as possible. But my preoccupation with detachment was the least of Patti's concerns as she tugged at me with funny, familiar stories where she and I were the main characters and were always the heroes. She kept drawing me in and talking to me like a sister. In those sessions, as in her daily, ordinary transactions, she was clear and unwavering in all she said, and although she positioned herself like a fighter, she welcomed and even loved all of my questions.

During one of my visits to her apartment, after we had finished the series of interviews I needed for the study, I got up the courage to ask her: "Can I videotape an interview?" By then, Patti looked very different. She had undergone the removal of her breast, and the side-effects of the radiation had caused a gross swelling of her left arm, had left her with just small patches of hair, and no eyebrows, and she had gained about 40 pounds. Yet, as all her close friends well knew, Patti was a living work of art, and so she shaved her head, painted and decorated her arm, and refused to wear her prosthesis. She also continued to teach, and to talk with me about her students and her dreams. Although the video recording was a personal venture unrelated to my research, I had a hunch that it might be valuable to Patti, me, and perhaps others. Nonetheless, I wrestled with the feeling that it might also be intrusive and even sensational. But she was not only agreeable, she took the project on as her own. She directed it, telling me the things she wanted everyone to know. I listened to painful and graphic monologues about the details of her surgery and treatment, her rage directed at the health care system, and her thoughtful insights about the role of friends and family during times of illness. Her posture took me by surprise—she was unusually formal, looking into the lens and speaking to an unidentified "public." Patti died later that year. This story has everything to do with this project, because it is in the writing of this essay that I have come to realize that this performance project, *Sweeping the Temple,* is about Patti and me, united in friendship and, once more, together on stage.

[sung]
Her face was painted . . .
        (I went to that dance class and I never left)
It was just very different from anything I'd seen . . .
        (I went to that dance class and I never left)
The movement was strong and the movement direct . . .
        (I went to that dance class and I never left)
The movement was harsh and it was with love . . .
        (I went to that dance class and I never left)

My research project about African American artists in higher education evolved over the next year. But as it neared completion, though I believed that it respectfully and quite vividly represented the experience of the teachers I interviewed, I felt like an outsider as I talked to these people who seemed somehow to have merged their scholarly and artistic lives. I hadn't performed in two years, having directed all my energy to this research. My artist-self felt the way I always do when I've gone through long, dry spells of musical celibacy, then gone to hear my colleagues in concert; me: stiff, tense, and awkward, them: on stage, illuminated in their spirit bodies, wings and all. In those moments, I'm sad, overjoyed, frustrated, inspired, depressed, exuberant, and confused, all at the same time. This was a clear sign that I needed to begin the process of integrating my performing with other aspects of my life.

As I worked on the book I kept wondering how this research might more accurately reflect me—the way I speak and think and function in the world. Revisiting the raw data, which consisted of many audio tapes, pages and pages of transcriptions, my journal notes, and memories of the interview sessions, I was struck by the fact that there seemed to be topics that kept surfacing. These artists/teachers shared so many ideas, although their angles on any particular subject were often quite different. I represented this diversity through the profiles of them that I crafted, and the identification and analysis of themes and topics that emerged. However, after I had designated data to those particular thematic areas, I was still left with delicious bits of wisdom, statements, parables, memories, advice, and words by these artist/teachers that did not seem to fit anywhere. At first, I felt that these "leftovers" seemed to render the analysis process untidy. Even more unsettling was that the words I read were quite clearly personal and directed to me as a Black woman. My participants were talking in that familiar way Black folks speak to each other in private—it's all in the subtext: the funny, coded, cryptic things we whisper under our breath, the way we raise our brows, roll our eyes, catch each others' glances, finish each others' sentences, and laugh real loud, certain that we know what each other means—fully aware that in this moment we're surely related. I loved it and was overwhelmed by the energy it gave me. Their voices spilled and bulged and seeped out of the margins of my data analysis. They talked about the slave trade and its effect upon us generations later. They talked about popular culture and community culture: Stevie Wonder, Marlon Brando, Rosa Parks, and their grandmothers. They talked about the difference between the ways Black mothers and White mothers discipline their children in public. They talked about God and spirituality. They talked about our assets and deficits, and some of the ways they learned about the importance of making social change.

I began to wonder just how private these talks really were or needed to be, and whether in fact, it was actually my own embarrassment at having my participants speak to me so intimately that was problematic. Did this familiarity make me less of a researcher? The question suggested my confusion around what it might mean to be a researcher. What happened next happened almost automatically. I started to gather up the mess and began grouping these comments. I realized that what I had was a series of short conversations. I was composing sound again. I was making songs and I could hear them in my head and it felt perfect. Best of all, I felt more like myself than I had at any other stage of the work. Making sure it flowed and that I produced just the right amount of tension, and the right number of pauses and accelerations as I made the "characters" enter and exit became my main concern. I had come to think of the book as a stage, a space with magnificent acoustics where voices would resonate. Most exciting was that the lines marking what was and wasn't permissible were becoming less defined. I played with the textures and colors and rhythms of these conversations. Was this one too angular? Too soft? Was that one bright enough? Fast enough? I was creating hushes and screams, drum rolls and cymbal crashes—places where they stood defiantly and delivered their lines, and places where they moved, tumbling in clumps, holding fast to each other. When I found gaps in these dialogues, I bridged them by introducing my own voice to theirs in the form of an "interviewer," commenting and questioning. My participants seemed to be speaking with each other, and my playwright-, poet-, and painter-selves were meeting the researcher.

Then, self-doubt crept in and I wondered whether I had crossed the line and had done something wrong—something unethical. The interviewer's voice was fictional, and although I had not tampered with any of my participants' words in the process of creating this conversation, they had clearly never spoken with each other, and in most cases had never even met. Furthermore, I wasn't sure that the permission they had granted me to use their interviews for my research included what I was doing here. I was on unfamiliar ground. But in the end, these conversations confidently took their places in the book and became what I called "riffs." I named them after the devices used by jazz improvisers, referring to short, catchy musical phrases periodically interjected to punctuate a musical idea. Bold and intense, they wound their way through the text. Nonetheless, I continued to struggle with my identity: How could I be a real researcher if, even when given the opportunity to enter the world of academic research, I couldn't resist the urge to make art: to play and have fun—to preach, scream, seduce, show off—to make something dazzling and fleeting—enjoyable to my ears and eyes and sense of humor and drama—to make myself laugh and cry—to brand something as uniquely my own?

From The Portrait to the Performance

The book was published and Patti's story was featured as one of four portraits that I developed from the interview data. However, that project was not complete and I knew it and the next step would be to breathe even more life into her portrait than I had been able to do through this narrative profile. *Sweeping the Temple,* a performance of my research, derives from several objectives. I had a desire to make Patti's experience more tangible to an audience—more sensual—more real. I wanted others to feel her tempo and anger and humor and vibrancy and sarcasm. I was also intent on honoring Patti, and one of my challenges would be to give her portrait a memorial quality while avoiding histrionics or any romanticizing of her death. Another concern was that of accessibility. It was important to communicate some key issues pertaining to the experience of at least this one African American teacher to an audience that might not read the published research.

It is impossible to discern where and when the research became art, nor is it desirable to do so. In most ways the research was always art. All that I bring to my process represents the part of me that makes what we call "art." In fact, I'm always risking and guessing and configuring and discarding and reconfiguring and retrieving and repeating and rehearsing and performing. But at some point, I realized that I simply wanted people to know Patti better. And so art holds no mysterious, majestic authority in this project. Rather, it is more of a way that I work than a thing that I make.

I entered into the new assignment of shaping my research into a performance by reading that narrative over and over again, highlighting parts that suddenly stood out for some reason. Sometimes, those passages had historical significance, or emotional or poetic value. Sometimes they simply sounded like Patti—that hasty, high-pitched, no-nonsense sonority. This point in the process was similar to the phenomenological interviewing I had done for the original study, where I searched for themes and topics from the raw data, only the highly polished profile I had crafted for the book now became the raw data for the performance. Still, I had no idea what I was looking for and so I stumbled rather clumsily through her profile. Initially, from this highlighted material, I had passages ranging from simple words and phrases to fascinating tales. I wanted to present a picture of Patti, but did not yet know what *sort* of picture it would be, nor did I want to decide *how* I would create it. I didn't even want to impose particular art forms on the work. Moving about in this dimly lit space with my arms outstretched and groping, I soon realized that there were two distinct bodies of text emerging. There were her stories, and there were my poems. It was the potential for abstraction and the possibility of raising questions and suggesting ambiguity and uncertainty that led to the emergence of the poems. Through grouped words and the omission of what I considered excessive language, it began to feel as though Patti's voice had timbre and volume, a voice that interrogated, punctuated, and offered clarification. I then took the groups of dynamic words and phrases I had identified and shaped into poems, and the lucid, precise sentences Patti made, and wove them together. Each aspect of her story became more solid and seemed to stand on its own. The work felt good as I read it.

Around the time I began to gain confidence in my selection of text I began to hear it performed in my mind. Realizing that Patti's voice would require layering, I decided to use taped excerpts as well as live ones. I was looking for depth—for reverberation—and I had a hunch that the mixing of live and prerecorded media would help achieve that. Although I didn't consciously decide how this would happen, I instinctively assigned the flowing, unbroken prose to be spoken on tape, while I reserved the poems for live delivery. Here is where I decided to sing the poems, and so they became songs. And to give them the quality that makes songs appealing to my ear, I interjected a repetitive phrase at key moments. This use of repetition and hence rhythm also reminds the audience that they are experiencing a performance and not merely a documentation of data.

[sung]
I don't remember saying I'm Negro
I don't remember saying I'm Colored
I don't remember saying I'm Black

I asked myself: What can I do to this material to give it appeal as a performance? I quickly found that its appeal would come through its dramatic success. This is a part of performance that has always been important to me. So, aside from using repetition to accomplish this, I needed to build in dynamic levels, which might be done in several ways. One way that I chose was through the impact of the information conveyed. There are statements Patti makes that shout out, while others are barely audible. The dynamic level here is an imagined one suggested by the intensity of the particular incidents of the stories themselves. Another way that dynamics would be achieved was through the layering and interaction of live and taped sound. Sonic texture is yet another device that was key to the success of the portrait. Here, "texture" refers to the visceral quality of the image conjured by sound—its rough, smooth, tangled, stringy, wet, dry, opaque, or thick feeling. I love working in these terms that are not usually used to describe sound, since the sense of hearing often feels inseparable from my other senses. In this case, I wanted the sounds to suggest things that could be touched with fingers or even tasted, and generally, I sought to bridge the sound experience with others. For this, I might play the violin, guitar, or small, hand-held percussion instruments. All of these devices helped construct an undercurrent in Patti's account—her thinking, her pulse—her deep self. . . .

[sung]
forever that is
forever the spirit that is
forever it is the spirit that is forever . . .

As I continued to work I gained a new appreciation for the ways my biases affected so many aspects of this work. In fact, by then it had become very clear to me that my findings had been a result of my attraction, or lack thereof, to certain data. However, this process of turning the data into a performance further removed Patti's words from her as I adopted and adapted them. She became even less of their owner as I carefully crafted moments of suspense, pauses at crucial points, and suggested emotions, perhaps ones that she hadn't even intended. For example, in a passage about the demands of teaching, how institutions often tend to treat people inhumanely, and the professional choices she faced, I vividly remember Patti's expression as being disturbed and animated, reflected in the inflection, volume, and speed at which she spoke. Yet, in performance I deliver her words in a detached, monotonous manner. At that particular point, it is the first time in the staged work that the live voice is not singing melodic lyrics, but reciting spoken words combined with an angular, lightning-quick, agile, and rhythmic vocal improvisation. It is the abrupt disruption of the expected that pulls the listener closer. I felt that if I delivered her monologue with intensity it would make it predictable, and even render it ineffective, and so I chose to create a distraction from her words, making them a backdrop and pulling the listener closer, into my rigorous vocalizing. It is an attempt to present Patti's words in a seemingly neutral way, while actually juxtaposing them with an unanticipated emotional device. My intention here is to present her professional dilemma, yet suggest a raw power that exists in such moments of decision.

These are some of the most exciting parts of the work—those moments when I measure and assess and weigh and compare. Most important is that these activities occur in the realm of the sensual and spiritual as well as the cognitive. Throughout the entire process I am giving myself permission to step inside and outside my body almost instantaneously, and experience the work through different lenses. The work is constantly scrutinized from every angle. I ask myself some crucial questions, such as, "have I interacted with the material sufficiently so as to have exhausted all that it requires of me?" In fact, Patti's portrait has a life of its own as a performance and from the beginning it reveals itself to me. So my question is whether I have responded to all aspects of that calling. Another question I ask as I attempt to remove myself even further from the work is, "does Patti's story feel complete and satisfying from the perspective of an audience member?" Here, the issue is about the ability of Patti's accounts to be thoroughly engaging. The other key question I ask is, "am I transformed by the process of performing this work?" That is probably the most crucial one because usually the other questions are answered in the affirmative if this one is. Yes, I need to be moved by my own work.

Finally, the map is complete and the work is ready for performance. It includes a combination of a taped monologue, live spoken and sung vocals, and a violin accompaniment. The lights are dimmed. The room is still. On tape, we hear Patti recalling childhood memories:

> [taped monologue]
> *I was an only child. At a point in time in my mother's life, she sang with Count Basie's band very, very briefly. My father was in two or three of Oscar Micheaux's films. One of them was called The Colored Underworld. We have pictures in our album of that movie, and I've seen clips of my father in that film on public TV. Also, my father's family was involved in what they called the Normal Schools in Washington, D.C., and the Underground Railroad. And I can even say, I mean, I don't know if it's anything to be proud of, but my great, great grandfather was the barber of Abraham Lincoln. There's a letter floating around in the family where when he left Abraham to have his own barber business, Abraham writes, "Yes, he was a good boy when he was in my service." I don't know who has that letter. Somebody has his hair, too, somewhere.*

The starkness of the lone, taped voice penetrating a silent room emphasizes this personal and precious act of remembering. Also, the quiet requires that the audience listen in a focused and uncomplicated way.

> [taped monologue]
> *I'd say we were middle class. My clothes were made for me when I was little. We had things and we didn't have to struggle because my father made money. He graduated from the Massachusetts Institute of Technology in 1916. My parents were invested in education. If you had an education, then that meant that you were a decent person, I guess. And if you didn't have an education, I'm not quite sure what that meant.*

She soon begins telling her coming-of-age stories and the narrative loses much of its initial reflective and even nostalgic quality. Here, I introduce the live voice to the taped one with a combination of very short poems and simple songs. Patti talks about some of the difficulties she experienced as a pregnant teenager and her determination to finish high school. She walks us through the brave moments of a young mother who has recently arrived in New England and is determined to make a good life for her daughter and herself. Trained as a dancer since she was very young, she addresses many of the social and emotional quandaries of performing professionally. She then enters a very different phase, as she speaks about her identity and evolution as a teacher, the nature of her relationships with colleagues, and her place in the academy. Again, the quality of the performance changes. The voices cease and the violin enters with a musical solo that positions itself slowly and solidly, then gradually picks up momentum, prompting yet another shift in the drama and paving the way for Patti's agile, uncompromising delivery:

> [taped monologue]
> *I do want to be in a university setting because I think you need all kinds of people in those kinds of institutions. I don't think that they can manipulate me and I don't think I can be held hostage by a job. And I think you need that type of person because you have a lot of lobotomized people in university settings. They're pretty much dead. They have stopped fighting for themselves and they have stopped fighting for anything that to me is of any kind of importance. You tell them to go jump in the lake and they'll go jump in the lake. They're robots. They're afraid for their jobs so they have gotten into a mold now that they can't get out of. This is White people, too. This is across the board. I don't care who it is. And that is a regimented kind of "Yessir, boss! I'll do whatever you say, boss. How long should I shuffle, boss?"*

Patti's singular voice from the original interviews I conducted has exploded and now demands space for her many voices, and that is what we hear. A multivocal quality takes hold and the live voice now periodically punctuates certain words to bring the audience closer to her pondering, her discomfort, the collision of her feelings, her impatience, her insistence. Increasingly, the textures warp, the rhythms become more complex, and the overall listening experience becomes thicker, more web-like, and simultaneously more engaging. At this moment, the live and taped voices both mirror and overlap each other and the vocal and instrumental sounds bump and collide with each other.

[chanted]
Dead . . .
Robots.
Dead.

Afraid.
Dead.
Yessir.
Lobotomized.
Robots.
Yessir.

The pace further escalates and concludes with Patti's monologue about the inevitable psychological traumas of racism, from which no one can escape.

[taped monologue]
We're in such a mess. I'm really concerned about us. But I want them to change things, too. See, I expect everybody to make changes. I really do. But my focus is people of color. And I don't treat my students any differently. I care for all of them, there's no doubt about it. Of course, I would prefer to be in an all Black classroom. Are we schizophrenic? In general, we have to be, I would assume. And I think we have to say that we're pathological. Black people are pathological. We are ill on a certain level. I think we have to acknowledge that because of what our history was. But it did damage to White people too. They're pathological also. They're sick. They're crazy too. We all have suffered because of this notion, this idea, this perpetuation of racism. That they feel so threatened by Black people—that they feel so threatened by us says to me there's something wrong. In other words, in order for me to celebrate who I am doesn't take away from who you are at all if you're a secure person. Now, if you're an insecure person, then for me to assert and celebrate who I am is going to make you scared and uptight. Yeah, I think it has made them ill too. You can't buy and sell people and think you're going to be all right. There's this idea about knowing things unconsciously as a group, a collective consciousness. There's some body-knowing that nobody can put their fingers on. Body-knowing. They're suffering too.

We hear the taped voice, speaking Patti's actual words from the interview. We also hear fragmented bits and pieces of words, interrupted thoughts, and jagged, hollow sounds. It is the live voice riding alongside the taped one in a racing improvisation that weaves both voices together in such a way that they become entangled and it is impossible to tell them apart.

[Sung, chanted, and improvised]
make . . . change . . . changes . . .(groan) makechanges. . . .are . . .
we . . . focus . . . fo. . . . schiz (ah!). . . o. . .
phre . . . nic . . . schiz . . . are you . . .(oh?) we . . .
make . . . we . . . patho . . . lo . . . pa . . . pa. .tho
pa . . . pa . . .
gical . . . path . . . olo . . . gi . . . pa . . . ca . . . sick . . .(m-m-m-m)sick
. . . sick suf . . .
suffer . . . su . . . su . . . su . . .(ahhhh)
ffered . . . sick. . . .sick . . . up . . .
tight . . . up. . . .tightuptight . . . arewe . . . are . . . we up . . .
white . . . up . . . whiteupsickup. . . .weblack . . . arewe (groan)

The live voice now overshadows the previously more prominent, linear account, and for the first time in the performance we hear the taped voice out of character. It is no longer in the forefront, in the role of descriptor. Instead, the taped monologue withdraws and concludes with a poem, pensive, spacious, and with sweet, slow, deep, audible vocal tones and breathing, a turn that metaphorically suggests the need for cognitive faculties to submit to the poetic abstraction of the spiritual realm. Completely overwhelmed with the imprint of racism on all of us, and what amounts to the human preoccupation with physicality, Patti concludes that our bodies have less significance than the importance we give them. She offers us her realization that the body is primarily useful for moving us around in the world, and that it is our inner self that is most precious and lasting.

[sung]
A shell.
It's just
A shell.
That's all it is.
The body
Is just
a shell,
Or a house,
Or a temple
Of the spirit.

From the Performance to the Pondering

My thinking is rooted in and shaped by my early training as an improvising musician. As I self-reflect, I see that I am always functioning as though I'm on the bandstand. What does this mean to my work as a researcher? It means that I continually apply many of the principles of jazz improvisation to my nonmusical engagements. I entered a powerful phase of this learning about 25 years ago, during which time pianist and educator Roland Wiggins (Lateef, 1981) taught me the value of exhausting ideas—of approaching a problem from its many possible solutions and methodically working them through. He used to talk about how he did this in his piano practicing and it always appealed to my desire to be fully immersed in my work. From the late John Carter (1985, 1986, 1988, 1989), composer and clarinetist, I learned that my imagination had retentive value—that it could be expressed and then referenced by others. During rehearsals he would give me written music that I thought was beyond my technical grasp. Once, when I mentioned that to him, he laughed and said that he had simply composed something for me to play that was similar to what he had heard me execute during one of my improvised solos from a previous performance. As part of violinist Leroy Jenkins' band (1977, 1978, 1984, 1992), I quickly discovered the unparalleled thrill of stepping out on a limb. His adventurous and highly personalized approach to improvising demanded that I, too, find my own style and be daring. With Steve Reid (1976), a drummer and mentor to many young, upcoming musicians, I began to build my muscles—to acquire stamina. Enthusiastically, the band would improvise for hours on end, then listen back so studiously to the taped recordings of our rehearsals.

Overall, although my learning has its foundations in the realm of sound, it directly translates into my functioning as a researcher. By virtue of the discipline required to learn this musical form, the principles I bring from this practice include capacities for three primary areas of functioning (Jenoure, 2000). I identify these as *interaction*, or the ability to shape and be shaped; *definition*, which entails the ongoing work of immediate assessment of myself, others, and the environment; and *transcendence*, an overriding of apparent limitations. However, the descriptions of the path I have taken to learn these principles are more than testimonies. They bear directly on *Sweeping the Temple* because, key to this project, from this community of musicians I came to realize that research is too narrowly defined, since what we do as musicians/artists is always research and is certainly scientific. Gratefully, I bring all of my lessons from all my wonderful mentors, applying the appreciation for rigor, dreaming, courage, and endurance, which I have been trained to treasure, to all aspects of my life's work.

> [sung]
> *Body*
> *Knowing*
> *Body-knowing . . .*
> *There's some*
> *BodyKnowing*
> *NoBody*
> *Can put their fingers on*

From the Pondering to the Possibilities

In summary, it is important to remember that *Sweeping the Temple* is alive. There is no demarcation indicating where the research ended and the performance began, since each facet was always related to the other. For simplicity's sake, one might say that it began with the phenomenological interview study, evolved to the stage when the conversational "riffs" were developed, then metamorphosed into a musical performance. Moreover, without apology, this performance no longer represents the range initially present in the early interviews I conducted with Patti, and even less the sum total of my participants' experience found in the original study. We cannot assume that Patti's story symbolizes anyone's experience but her own. In that way, it is necessary to think of the performance as having a life related to, yet really quite separate from, the research. To turn research into art, I had to first let go of expectations that this project would in any way replicate or even represent my initial study, although, certainly, the art is intended to report some aspects of it. In the case of this work, the performance became a vehicle for further examining specific details of Patti's experience. In fact, the notion of performing the data became a research project in its own right—one where I wanted to find out at least the following: What methods and tools might I use to tell Patti's story? To what degree might I maintain the intention of the original research? What devices might I use to suggest aspects of the findings that I identify as important, yet not feel the need to represent them in any literal way?

There are endless possibilities for the merging of research and art. What seems so exciting is that although for me, research and art are always, and have always been, inseparable, recognizing their close relationship marks an opportunity for promoting more healthy, holistic functioning for myself and hopefully for other practitioners and audiences. It reminds me to identify my art as research, and to acknowledge the debt that research owes to the imagination. In addition to the fact that there are numerous ways that other artists and researchers approach this paradigm, even the process that I have described would be quite different if I were to undertake it again. Following the completion of this performance, I immediately began plans to integrate Patti's story into a larger work. It promises to access other data about artists/teachers from the published study and apply the use of puppets, dance, and photographic slides, as well as the video recording of Patti I conducted four years ago, which to date, for emotional reasons, I have yet to view. What lies beyond this is unclear. At the moment all the voices from this study seem to be quiet. Does that mean that *Sweeping the Temple* is complete? Only time will tell. Until then, I rest in the fact that my hand has pushed a door that now swings wide open. Patti's portrait, like a curtain, billowing and transparent, drapes from overhead and fully covers the opening of the entryway. I'm walking through it.

References

Books:

Jenoure, T. (2000). *Navigators: African american musicians, dancers, and visual artists in academe.* Albany: State University of New York Press.

Lateef, Y. (1981). Introduction In *Repository of scales and melodic patterns.* Amherst, MA: Fana Music.

Seidman, I. E. (1991). *Interviewing as qualitative research.* New York: Teachers College Press.

Music Recordings:

Carter, J. (1985). *Castles of Ghana.* New York: Gramavision Records.

Carter, J. (1986). *Dance of the love ghosts.* New York: Gramavision Records.

Carter, J. (1988). *Fields.* New York: Gramavision Records.

Carter, J. (1989). *Shadows on a wall.* New York: Gramavision Records.

Jenkins, L. (1977). *Lifelong ambitions.* Milano, Italy: Black Saint Records.

Jenkins, L. (1978). *Space mind, new worlds, survival America*. Milano, Italy: Black Saint Records.
Jenkins, L. (1984). *Urban blues*. Milano, Italy: Black Saint Records.
Jenkins, L. (1992) *Live*. Milano, Italy: Black Saint Records.
Reid, S. (1976). *Nova*. Brooklyn, New York: Mustevic Sound Records.

CHAPTER 6

If I Could Have Said It, I Would Have

DONALD S. BLUMENFELD-JONES

There are so many choices, so many ways to begin and no good way to begin. I face a difficulty. I am asked to tell you about the making of art, about what I do and about what you might do and what you might know from me that might, if not ease your way, make it more visible. I'm asked to link up art and research. The last, that's the easy one, the one about which I could talk and talk, write and write, working out the details, laying out the terrain. But that will not help you do the art. And that is the one thing about which I feel tongue-tied and reluctant.

For what can I say that would make any sense? Nothing I would tell you could be copied and used. It could be experimented around, but to experiment you would have to look at/experience the art and, if you so chose, imitate and alter, find out about its workings by trying to do it. Nothing I can say, so I think, can lead you toward that understanding which will only flow from your doing. Put down this essay, this book! Get to work, your own work, now!

This is an essay, therefore, about the impossibility of speaking, about the impossibility of art. This is an essay about the impossibility of speaking about the impossibility of art which makes everything possible but of which we cannot speak. This is an essay about the love of art, a love whose name we speak but whose naming in the way of doing we do not know.

But I will speak and in that speaking hope (within the boundaries of my reluctant tongue) that something may emerge which you will find useful, helpful or some sort of -ful. I'll begin with an anecdote about my dancing years, do some of that theoretical work of which I wrote, and then try, try to give you a sense of how I think about art and doing. Will it help you do it? I don't know, but I'll try.

Many years ago the company with whom I danced, the Phyllis Lamhut Dance Company, participated in a federal program, "Dancers in Schools." In this program we would work in a school for a two-week period, teaching dance and performing and helping teachers see how dance could support academic work. Our challenge was to devise classes which both helped the students understand and do their academic work more successfully *and* maintained the integrity of the art. Some of my colleagues resented this aspect of the work as they felt dance was being made second-class and their whole interest was in the art, not the art as tool for something else. For my part I thought the challenge both worthy and enjoyable. My central concern was seeing that the instrumental use of the art was supported by the quality of the art, rather than feeling a need to choose one or the other. I am still convinced of this possibility.

This same challenge exists for those of us trying to meld artwork with education research and it raises questions for us. Do the arts enhance educational research? Do the arts provide a unique contribution to educational research and, if so, what is that contribution? Do we preserve the integrity of the art over the research or vice versa or do we find a negotiated peace between them? Several years ago Elliot Eisner (1995) addressed these questions, listing a number of visual and literary works and films having to do with schools. He went on to write,

> The works I have cited are not normally thought of as examples of research; they are regarded as personal creations sprinkled liberally with metaphor and displaying points of view that are vague and subjective. But this distinction between research and nonresearch is too sharp. . . . [T]he question of what counts as research . . . turns on our conception of understanding. . . . [T]he works I have cited help us to understand because their creators have understood and had the skills and imagination to transform their understanding into forms that help us to notice what we have learned not to see. (p. 3)

Eisner was describing a distinction often made between research and artworks: artworks are "personal creations sprinkled liberally with metaphor and . . . are vague and subjective." Research works are, by implication, impersonal non-creations, which are concrete and objective.

I would argue that these distinctions can't, upon examination, be fully supported. Education research is not impersonal at all. Rather, it should be understood, like art, as a "personal creation." This is because it does not exist in some extra-corporeal form plucked from the ether by the researcher. A particular researcher enacts a particular practice to produce a particular product for personal reasons. Many of these products do not count as "art" but this does not make them any less personal, even if the practice in use is meant to be highly impersonal. Further, researchers choose modes of research and make of them what they will and enact the various modes in better or worse manners, according to the canons of those modes. And what could be more concrete and objective than a painting or a dance: real paint, real surface, real people doing real movements? Of course, what is meant by "vague and subjective" is that the artist's perspective cannot be judged to be wrong or right (because it is accused of being merely subjective or personal), nor can the artist's perspective be, necessarily, simply communicated (therefore it is accused of being vague). There may be varying interpretations about the meaning of an artwork and, for research, there is meant to be only one interpretation of it. However, if research were simple and straightforward upon examination there would be no disagreements among researchers into a specific area and we know that there are. No research, even quantitative research, is free from the interpretive and the personal. Additionally, it is now well established that language, even technical language, is replete with metaphors. This suggests that even distinguishing the kinds of language for each endeavor is a weak distinction.

If the distinctions made are specious, then it would be correct to say that education research and art making are the same endeavor in different modes. Indeed, my approach to these questions is to conceptualize how research is much more like art than researchers might care to admit. In so doing, I happily accept the notion that my artwork/research is a "personal creation" which is "sprinkled liberally with metaphor and displaying points of view that are vague and subjective," and I eschew the myth of research being truthful and objective in some ultimate way. Further, from this point on, I will no longer discuss the research aspects of my project but, rather, the art aspects of the project as legitimate forms of data analysis.

In light of the above the appropriate questions fall to the art-side of thinking. What kind of art is this? Is this, in my estimation, good art? What am I feeling? What is my experience? What do I now know? The "what" of what I know will vary according to the subject of the art (education, marriage, racism, sexuality, or whatever) but my concern will be with the art which confronts me and which I confront. As a critical theorist I am also concerned with the place of art in the socio-economic-cultural context, but in thinking of art as education research I place those concerns, temporarily, out of court. While art is socially produced and embeds class, race, ethnicity, and gender issues as well as issues of social justice, compassion, and ethics, when I am thinking about *this* piece of art, I am noticing it as art and taking it on those terms.

Notice, in the above, that I have not mentioned education research, except in passing. Whatever ways we construe art to make contributions to human existence in general can be found, or not, in contributions to education research, as a species of human existence. Our judgments will be based not on "art as education research" but, rather, as I have already written, on our responses to the particular artwork, on whether or not we find the particular work worthy from an art point of view. While it may be that our "worth" judgments may have mixed into them concerns about what the work may mean for an education issue (in this case), we are not, I would argue, actually judging the work on that basis. We are, rather, responding to the work of art as art and then thinking about its implications for its subject. Perhaps I should state this differently: I think we *should* first think about the work as art rather than concerning ourselves with its educational value, for when we attempt to determine the value of the research before we have actually engaged with the research (the art) on its own terms (as art) there seems no viable way of knowing whether or not that work is contributing to, as Eisner has it, our understanding.

My concern is focused primarily on the artwork's aesthetic qualities. When I have been delighted with something it is due to the aesthetics which are working to bring about, in me, some experience, some immediacy of insight, some FEELING which, in the immediacy of the moment, cannot be described but can only be. When I have not been delighted it is because I have not felt anything but have to use my mind to parse out the event. Intellectual engagement must be grounded in and set up by another engagement which occurs "below the threshold" as it were, interiorly and in a way that may be inexpressible in language but is, nevertheless, powerful. In this present project, therefore, I am concerned with the practice of art rather than education research, concerned with the kinds of experiences it is possible for my audience to have: not what they can learn but, rather, what they can possibly feel and how I can structure the situation so that they feel something, rather than nothing.

Let me give an example. Recently at a performance piece installation, an artist had created an naturalistic/human technology environment consisting of a large hollowed out log with a floating garden in it and various log sconces and objects displayed around the outer edge of the room, some on the wall, some set in piles of stones. He had integrated a set of bodily function monitoring devices and immersed himself in the water of the floating garden, connected to the monitoring devices which were, in turn, connected to pumps which moved water in small waterfalls and fountains in the sconces. His bodily functions controlled the environment. The setting was beautiful and attracted me. My host, on the other hand, wanted to explain the work to me by discussing the intellectual thought behind the art: the artist's desire to question the relationship between humans, their technology, and their environment. I found such talk intrusive. If experiencing the environment could not provide the understanding, then what was the use? If everything had to be explained so that a univocal meaning would emerge, then why not just tell me what the meaning was. However, for me, since art is experience, whatever was there for me was found in my immediacy in the presence of the art. John Cage (1973, p. 20), the twentieth-century composer, said it even more succinctly: "If I could have said it in words, I would have."

That is the way I feel. I cannot tell you what the poetic work I have done means. I would not dare and do not know. That is not the point. The point is for experience to emerge, to happen for you. My fixation is on the materials, on thinking through the sound and words, the music, which makes the words worth reading, and thinking about my ideas about the situation in the light of materials. Style, but not empty style.

In the present work[1] upon which this essay is based I have made a set of literary objects (poems, anecdotal stories, prose poems, autobiography) rather than a report upon the project. In this mélange of writing I hope to provide, at all turns, poetic language/music. And the myriad of literary objects ensconced within are not neatly put together in a rational, linear way, each one following the one upon the other. I am not concerned with coherence, with the whole object "adding up," but, rather, with the thoughts/feelings you have as you encounter the opportunity to experience/think/feel.

I work in two ways. First, there must be, for this kind of work, substantive intellectual groundwork. In the case of this project the intellectual work dealt with a Navajo Bureau of Indian Affairs (BIA) school curriculum development project.[2] Margaret Lindauer and I have analyzed our field data from three perspectives: postcolonial theory (Ms. Lindauer's specialty), discourse analysis/metaphor analysis, and Bourdieuean field analysis (these last two are my specialties). My understanding of the project through this work provided the basis upon which to develop the artwork. The poetry and so forth provide what is absent from the other forms of analysis: feelings and direct experience. Further, I discovered aspects of the situation not discoverable in other ways.

Second, I work scatteredly. That is, I think of images, I present myself with images and language, and I "see" what strikes me, what seems to have potential to go somewhere. I often did this when choreographing. I would have a theme (sign language, Indian women left behind while the men went to war, sneakers, death) but might not know what I wanted to do although I had dancers with whom to work. I would present myself with mental images of them dancing the theme, doing this and doing that until some image struck me with the possibility of being developed. Then I would go into the studio by myself and begin to work out the movements I had already seen, feel through the tension between the nascent ideas and the organic feeling motion that was emerging as I worked. The emphasis was always on the motion, trusting that the "ideas" would only be developed and understood through the materials at hand. The materials and their manipulations would reveal, for me, the "meaning" (if I can use a word which I always use carefully). I would not start with a full idea of the meaning. I might not even have a sense of how the whole dance was coming together until well down the road of the work. Just as novelists talk about their characters taking over the work and directing the development of the novel, so, too, the motion and the feelings drove my work and allowed me to "work out" the meaning that was not yet apparent. The same can be said of this poetry project.

You may rightly ask: How do I know which images are worth developing? I can only say that I feel it. I see movement (or words) evolving, see the whole dance (or poem) in a certain way although through the working process much else happens. I keep referring back to that image and the theme, seeing how the images have altered the theme and how the theme must be brought to bear upon the images. The receptive beholder may encounter the initial image which animated the work in the first place, and in that beholding seek a message or answer a question which is there for him or her. What those reasons/messages/questions are I cannot say, nor need I. It is enough to provide the possibility, which is also my possibility, which enlivens me and enlivens the work. But I do leave it to the receiver to sew the elements together in ways that may help him or her. Even with me, I don't know what the meaning is absolutely or necessarily. And if I did, I would not and could not impose it upon the receiver.

This is not to say that every meaning is acceptable. Certainly there must be some resonance between the presented images and the meaning. Otherwise what's the point, for me, of presenting this work at all? My initial meaning offers the possibility, through a particular constellation of meanings, of the receiver making meaning. So not any interpretation will do, but there are many meaningful experiences that are not mine and cannot be mine.

How do I actually write? I place myself in a "poetic" state of mind. Does that sound pretentious? I don't mean for it to do so and yet I know of no other way to state it. I prepare myself to hear words, experience images, listen for music. I cannot stress strongly enough my devotion to words, to their sound as well as their meanings. For me that is what poetry is. It is the immediacy of experiencing the poem itself, the sensuality of the thing blended with meaning.

On the other hand, I must be careful here. Dancers are notorious, so Alwin Nikolais (Siegel, 1971) felt, for only wanting to dance. Given their choice they would have lots of movement to do that was complex and interesting, not knowing the value of silence, of stillness. They only want to "shake their butts." This is not devotion to the artistic statement but to self-indulgence. Artists, on the other hand, are "champion choosers," people who can select with an astute mind/eye between that which will serve and that which is mere noodling about. What can be said of dance can be said for any of the arts. We must be choosy, first and foremost. As W. H. Auden would have it (personal communication, poetry workshop leader, 1968), the poet should write the poem, read the poem, and then get rid of everything in the poem which he or she especially liked. Probably that material is too close to the poet's self and not necessarily good for the poem, which must take precedence. One must be ruthless and tear up the offending page. To leave this material in is to care for oneself and not for the art

It is not enough to think of the materials. Structure is highly important. Words do not exist separately from each other but bump up against each other and the differing ways of organizing them changes their bumps and our subsequent experience of them. So, one must play, all the time play with the words, be open to various arrangements and allow, indeed allow, the words, the structure to emerge in that state of play. Is playing something that can be taught? Not the urge, but the discipline of play. Play is discipline, a strange concatenation of ideas but necessary to each other.

Exemplary of this play is the way I created the poems and other works. The words you encounter in the piece are not from the dataset. I portray a "showdown" in "The Rooms of the Meeting" which did not actually happen at one time or in one way. Rather, I have compressed my impression of many events into this one "event." I have imported many experiences (stopping in Gallup, New Mexico, visiting Cherokee, North Carolina, driving across the reservation in August, viewing *Cat Ballou*), which have ostensibly nothing to do with this set of events. They are used because they impacted my response to this event, becoming pertinent to the project.

"Hogan Dreams" is an example of how I worked on this project. During my experience of the meetings, hogans became a pervasive image as the meeting house, for the school is in the style of the hogan, the plans for the new buildings are in the style of hogans, the assistant principal has a custom-built home in the style of a hogan, and I have seen many hogans as I have driven across the Navajo Reservation.

Hogan Dreams

I – The Hogan Dreams

The hogan—eight-sided wonder of the world—
knot of geography drawing the earth
through its delicate threads.

The hogan—axis of the spinning earth—
rough-hewn and mud daubed,
settled into the dust of the desert.

The hogan—Can the hogan be this axis—
so small and heavy under
the scudding sun?

The hogan—draws the sun
through that knot,
makes the sun work for its ends, is worked by the ends of the sun.

The hogan—an invention of time
so old, no origin is known
but reverence follows in a minute.

The hogan—in this life
so much to do,
to know and here, in the hogan, life is lived.

A life is lived—in the hogan—
a life known by those whose life within the
walls of the hogan streams out

into the desert
and the high pastures where, in summer,
the sheep graze,
the horses neigh,
the dogs bark,
the people breathe
of Navajo.

II – The Assistant Principal Dreams (of a home)
Or the postmodern hogan

Another hogan—this the invention of a mind—
Knowing of the West
(no north, no south, no east).

Another hogan—hoping to find
In the eight walls,
Amongst their smooth, roughed out timbers

Another hogan—this of the mind
Of the liver in these walls
Delivered from his own destiny.

Another hogan—rich and replete
With new ideas, the hogan
Updated, delivered from time.

Another hogan—rich with water, ladders,
Stone and gleaming steel, beyond the hopes of
The hogan dwellers who see this edifice.

Another hogan—this one owned—
Can you own a hogan
Or are you owned by the hogan?
As your life is made
Within the story-telling of your fires
Made with wood and stone and, here,
Made with another's money.

Another hogan—stealing the desert land,
Sweeping up its dust inside and
Fortified with heavy walls—no streaming here.

Another hogan—anti-hogan—
Another universe without the sun
To guide and intervene its life.

III – The Principal Dreams (of a school)
Or the institutional hogan

Many Hogans—the invention of a mind
Which hopes to transform
The mind of the people.

Many hogans—massive rooved
Green and tan,
The colors of the desert perhaps.

Many hogans—Careering
Through the sky,
Linked and flowing as no sun could.

Many hogans—the budding pictures of a dream
Held by one for the people
In hogans, understood by whom?

Many hogans—restoring the people's dreams
Forgotten, for there are no hogans,
Or they are desert hidden.

These many hogans cannot be hidden,
Nor will they be as
They monument the moment.

Many hogans—is it their eight-sided nature
That makes them hogans
Or the people inhabited by them?

Many hogans—imitation of hope
For living among the hogan
That is lived in by the people.

A hogan, of course, is central to the Navajo people. I recall that when I was in the primary or perhaps elementary grades, I had a book about the Navajo and the only lasting image I have of that book is a drawing of a Navajo man (older) dressed in Navajo garb (the band around the head, the pants, the boots, and so forth) standing in front of a hogan in what I now know to call Monument Valley. Hogans are a way of organizing living space in a sacred manner, in accord with the world. Hogans, their structure, their orientation to geography, encapsulate much of the meaning of being Navajo. The hogan structure is used by some Navajo educational theorists as the image through which to think what a Navajo education might be.

Hogans, geography, and weather (living in the geography) emerged as central themes early on, although I didn't know why. I only knew that images/words of weather and geography captured my imagination and that hogans were distinctive and also seemed important. Not until I began work on the hogan poem did the relationship between these three begin to appear. Hogans, geographic harbingers of fate, and living in the high country in which one feels exposed to the weather so much more immediately (no cities to modify it) became preeminent in my mind and seemed to speak to the curriculum project experience. However, even as I write this I fear the reductionism of these statements. There is more to this than I can ever say and explaining is destructive to the poetry.

Hogans, as I have written, became a powerful, meaningful image for me. It began with thinking about the assistant principal's primary reason for building his new home in the style of a hogan: to have some of that spirituality in his own life. He has departed significantly from the traditional hogan. In the middle of the home, he has installed a story-telling pit, which contains a primitive looking fireplace and is entered by climbing down a ladder. Additionally, the hogan is two-storied, accessed again via a ladder. There is a running stream inside the house and the rooms of the home are arranged around the outer edge of the hogan. The home is ostentatious, both in its size and in its pretensions to spirituality. This is not to say that the assistant principal has pretensions. He seeks to bring spirituality into his life through this architecture. I encountered this hogan in the late afternoon of the first meetings we had at the school, which had been extremely frustrating, and I felt ready to explode with my frustration.

Ironically there are almost no Navajos that could afford to build such a home. When you drive past a Navajo home you see an ordinary house (block construction in most cases) and a hogan. The hogan is reserved, I believe, for spiritual ceremonies and practice. It is not, now, used as primary living quarters as far as I know. The ironies, then, of the assistant principal's hogan home is the wealth required to build it (in the midst of a region that is quite poor) and, the fact that his co-optation of Native American ways, as summarized through his various architectural inventions, runs counter to the conditions in which he is living. He is able to afford this home because he lives off a Bureau of Indian Affairs (BIA) salary. He is, in a sense, teaching the Navajos how to be Navajo. This is not to say that he is consciously doing so, but the lessons are there and they surely set him apart from the community (to which he belongs, in part, by dint of having married a Navajo woman who teaches at the school). As I began to write "Hogan Dreams" I discovered that his home had a connection with my frustrations and, surrounded by various hogans and images of hogans and the ironies of all this. It is little wonder that I selected the poem's particular images as part of the work.

I have just given an interpretation of the poem "Hogan Dreams." I did not know that this was the meaning of the poem (for me) until I began the poem. Once I discovered it, I also realized that this could not have been known to me through other forms of analysis. Those forms are intellectual, mental work and what I have found is not intellectual; it is feeling, bodywork found through the play of poetic images. The intellect does not deal with feeling through poetic images although I can now, having discovered the feeling, analyze it with intellectual means. Only in poetry could the feeling for hogans, in all their multifarious forms, find any scope for this kind of development, at least as I see it. But I am cautious about these distinctions. I do not make a full divide between feeling (the body) and intellect (the mind) but, rather, emphasize the ways in which the body is more featured in this work than the mind. And I do mean "the body" because feeling, for me, is felt bodily. It is, as Robert Frost (personal communication, Julian Moynihan, 1965) once said, when asked what made a poem work for him, "It makes my toes twinkle."

How did I proceed? I was, as usual, riding my bike with my dog, knowing that I wanted something about hogans in the work. I had entertained this thought without development. Now I put my poet's mind to the work and, after viewing various words, there it was, the opening line, "The hogan—eight sided wonder of the world." From where did that line come? I don't really know. It was just there and sang to me. As I began work on the opening verses I decided to structure the poem according to eightness to honor the hogan's structure: there would be eight verses to each section. I knew that I was disturbed by the assistant principal's home. I knew that would be part of the poem. Then I realized that his hogan wasn't of the Navajo hogans but "another hogan" altogether and that gave me insight into how to proceed, imagistically. Only later did I remember that the plans for the new school were modeled on hogans. And I had my poem. Certainly my work wasn't done but the structure was there within which to play.

Play is the crux of the matter: at play among materials and the ideas. "Postmodern hogan" and "institutional hogan" appealed to my taste for structure and amusement (I find those images amusing and I am hoping that when you read the titles for each section and read " . . . or the postmodern hogan" you smiled with me—perhaps not and that is all right too). "The postmodern hogan" because it is a pastiche of various traditions and, therefore, honoring none of them but rather raiding them. "The institutional hogan" because the new buildings are to be monumental structures that have nothing to do with hogans and yet are meant to impress on multiple levels (luxurious new buildings in a non-luxurious traditional form). I am "explaining" all this so that you can see some of the ways in which I proceeded with the work.

I began with my concerns over writing this and I end with them. What have I done? Has my talking damaged the poetry/literary objects? I dislike talking about art although I do engage in it. But I recall that each time I have seen *Lawrence of Arabia* and *A Chorus Line* I have been speechless and have not wanted to talk. Other people are chattering on about the movie, the show, and I am stock still in my mind/body, feeling what I have just felt, remembering moments that arrested me, not wanting the feelings to end and having to re-enter the "real" world. But which is the "real" world? And where shall I live? What makes that experience any less real? Does it make me live my life any differently? Does that matter? Have I told you anything useful?

Notes

1. The artwork which I am calling a "literary object" is actually a 50-minute performance piece to be read/performed by a solo performer. The script is designed to be presented in both live format and videoed format. What you see on the CD accompanying this book are excerpts from a video designed performance. This presentation of the work is only meant to give a flavor of the whole. It is not meant to present the "most central" parts of the performance or the parts which I think are highlights. No one can say, for a particular viewer/experiencer, what will be most vital for that person. Please view the performance in this spirit.

2. The curriculum development project which is the basis for the artwork was being enacted for a single BIA school on the Navajo Reservation. The project was funded by a grant from the National Endowment for the Humanities (NEH). The two principal investigators (the people who administer the grant money and determine what activities will be done) were a university-based arts professor and the principal of the school. Initial meetings were held at the school in late fall 1998 over a two-day period and included community members, the small design team (consisting of two principal investigators; a curriculum specialist; a technology specialist, who did not attend the first meetings; myself as the project evaluator; my graduate assistant and doctoral student, Margaret Lindauer; the assistant principal of the school; and a Navajo graduate student I had invited into the project) and the school faculty. All subsequent meetings were held on the university campus (five one and one-half day meetings) during spring 1999 and were attended by the design team, selected school faculty, selected community members, and outside specialist

consultants. The intent of the project was to develop a curriculum framework which would become the basis for applying for subsequent money whose purpose was to allow the framework to become a developed curriculum and then be enacted. The project was successful in that the subsequent money was awarded to the school. The research (which is the basis for the performance script) was conducted by Margaret Lindauer and myself. The data consists of extensive and thorough field notes and verbatims (direct quotes in the field notes), documents from the project, and journals kept by the participants.

References

Buber, M. (1970). *I and Thou*. (W. Kaufmann, Trans.). New York: Scribners.
Cage, J. (1973). *Silence*. Middletown, CT: Wesleyan University Press.
Eisner, E. (1995). What artistically crafted research can help us to understand about our schools. *Educational Theory, 45*(1) 1–6.
Siegel, M. B. (Ed.). (1971). *Nik: A documentary*. New York: Dance perspectives.

CHAPTER 7

Imagine, Inventing a Data-Dancer

G. W. RASBERRY

If it were not a process, there would be no surprise.
—Greene, *Releasing the Imagination*

Part 1, "Dreaming the Boat in the Air"

Jennifer. Sasha. Brant. Kelly. Kevin. Julia. Robyn.[1] Seven children: seven composers. Singers. Songmakers. Artists. Forward-leaning. Energy-driven. Dynamic. Excitable. Open. Incorrigible. Keen. Wonderfully malleable. Musicmakers.

We meet on Thursday afternoons. We create. We compose. Laugh. Collaborate. Improvise. Invent stuff. Share ideas without embarrassment. We act as though we know what we're doing. Beautifulcrazy notes fill the spaces. No one mentions the word curriculum. No one wonders when the period will end. Eight-year-old kids never fail to astonish me with their capacity for creativity, their lust for adventure and learning. I weave and bob among them each week, hanging on for the ride, loving the trip. Ask us how our (re)-search is going and we'll tell you we're busy dreaming the boat in the air. . . .

I'm the butterfly now. You sing when my wings move . . . .

. . . but the shack was empty
except for juniper boards
and Uncle Jim in the corner
beside an oil-drum furnace
reading Robert Service . . .

This stanza is from a poem called "How Boats are Built" by Carl Leggo (1999, p. 20) in which the poet's uncle, a boat builder, *appears* to be making little progress in his work. This poem speaks well to the journey I have embarked upon with these Grade 3 students. The poem continues,

What have you been doing
all winter? I asked.

Just sitting in this corner, he said,
watching the alders grow in the ice,
trying to stay warm, dreaming
the new boat in the air.

It's almost time to call
the woods together. Soon.
Already I've sailed a sea or two.

Uncle Jim in his shack. The children in their classroom. And me, somewhere in between. All of us dreaming. Imagining. Improvising. Searching. Researching. Works-in-progress. Works-in-process, living with and leaning on process. Moving backward and forward. Living in-between: seeking a place where the known and the unknown might touch. Learning to do imagination's work: realize dreams.

Dreaming the new boat in the air: this, for me, is a lovely and powerful image which helps to convey some of the true complexity of the creative process and, in turn, the research which, in this case, attempts to trace its beautifully serpentine course. Both require a considerable amount of faith. The poem about boat-building, and the "poetry" of the children who work and sing and play together help create an "interpretive location" (Sumara, 1996) that enables us to bring dreaming and researching together. Juxtaposition is, of course, one of the provocative services that poetry offers. The poet and the poem often bring what might be considered disparate elements and images together so that each might be considered differently: dreaming research, research dreaming. Even research and poetry, themselves, make for an interesting juxtaposition: the poetry of research. The poetry of research—a poetics of research—holds the capacity to bring the lines and the lives together. The lines that run through our lives and the lives that run through our lines. We sometimes watch, sometimes wait for pattern and sense to emerge, or perhaps we build pattern and sense one word at a time. The line is drawn, the line is written. Words fall out and, like poetry, form patterns, tiny at first. We attempt to follow. It's a tentative, tenuous process. As writer Jeanette Winterson describes it, "the rope is hand produced; the writer [researcher] makes it as she walks it" (1996, p. 161).

Does writing follow research or does research follow writing? Many of us live with the notion that our research writes us. That is, research dictates writing, it tells us what to write once we have finished researching. Others, myself included, embrace writing (process) in their methodological and epistemological wrestlings with research. They follow their writing to find out what it is they are researching. As Laurel Richardson, a writer and professor of sociology, offers, "writing is not just a mopping-up activity at the end of the research project . . . it is also a way of knowing . . . a method of inquiry" (1994, p. 516).

Research dreaming. Dreaming research. So our waiting and watching (sitting in the corner, trying to stay warm) belies much of the invisible work that goes on, this work of fashioning something from nothing. The process of enacting dreams invokes others working words, words that help do the work of creativity, words that inform our talk of creativity. These include words like vision and envision, intention and in-tension. Attention and attending. These are words that help us articulate the work of enacting dreams or visions or goals—or research. For me, they draw the dreamy word creativity toward the tangible, toward the solidity of the word "creating." How does creating relate to creativity? Can they live together in the same sentence? Yes: "How do we learn to create conditions in our lives that enable us to live creatively?" "How do we learn to create conditions in our creativity that enable us to engage in acts of 'doing,' like writing songs, making music, building boats, writing research, improvising a solo, teaching in the moment, collaborating with a challenging colleague?" These are issues that intrigue me. I am interested in the ongoing conversation—the invitation—that compels us to articulate the ways we might attempt to live well with the compelling uncertainty that being creative seems to involve.

I carry this conversation and these questions forward into my practice, into my theories, into my dreaming. They inform my work as a researcher, as a musician, as a teacher, as a learner, as a writer, as a parent—as a person who seeks to live poetically and creatively in the world with others. I am carried forward by desire and also by fear, by questions that I hope can and can't be answered. I am moved along by the richness and privilege of my own experiences as well as by the ambivalence and uncertainty that so often trouble my attempts to live creatively in the world.

I play and work with children in schools. I play and work with their teachers and also with those who seek to become (their) teachers. I attempt to live with all of these human beings in the space where learning seems so easy and so impossible. This research project seeks to create conditions that will enable me to discover ongoing ways to nurture the spark that fires questions that have to do with creativity and pedagogy, improvisation and composition in people's lives.

It's almost time to call the woods together. Soon.

It's a small, small school, this place of particulars where I've decided to begin to formally dance data. Three classrooms, no office, no gymnasium, no principal. Two teachers, several teaching aides, and fifty or so kids. Kindergarten to Grade 3 students fall into multi-aged groupings. The school is designated within the local school district as a "Family School." It's located in a small, rural village with a wonderful schoolyard that runs off to become field and trees beyond the farm fence. There's music and laughter. The children are easy to love.

I happen to live in this small village. I spend part of every Friday morning at the school.[2] For the past few years, we've been gathering together to sing and make music. Most Fridays the whole school gets together, other times we gather in smaller groups. It's only recently that I've begun to meet on Thursday afternoons with a very small group of students to sing and play and improvise and talk. Jennifer, Sasha, Brant, Kelly, Kevin, Julia, and Robyn are teaching me to dance . . . . data.

A curiosity for learning helps draw the line that keeps our lives connected. We work and play with words and notes and spaces. Beyond that we're not certain what names to attach to the things we do. We may end up writing skits or songs. We may not. The gift available to us is having the luxury to simply be together. To simply be. Like most groups in classrooms, we share a potential space of pedagogy. The question of what becomes pedagogical is open to (our) interpretation. That is, we make it up. In our case, the particulars of our shared experience that come into greatest relief are the pedagogical relations that emerge from an often precarious and porous set of roles we share as learners who are purposefully engaged in creative acts of improvisation. At some level, this is no different than, say, a math lesson or an art activity. Teaching and learning are themselves improvisational. At another level, however, we have chosen to purposefully blur many of the recognizable features we have come to call school and classroom, teacher and student/learner, teaching and learning. This is because the business of play is our curricular guide on Thursday afternoons. I am a teacher, yet not a teacher. (And, significantly, I am not *their* teacher.) To these students, I am a musician—the guy who shows up Friday mornings to sing and make music with them. And, conversely, to me these students are simply kids who sing and play. Together, we are not bound by any curriculum yet neither are we eschewing the curriculum. In no way would we consider our time together extracurricular, that pejorative and dismissive phrase too often used to brand anything not considered fundamental or basic to the curriculum of accountability. We are playing at the work of curriculum, engaging in playful curricular acts as we learn to develop a language for the exchange of musical and creative ideas.

In an interesting way, this curricular freedom enables me to more easily enact and talk about pedagogy as a kind of music-making. In turn, questions of how we might learn to "make music" together take on a certain interpretive potency when they are nested within larger questions that begin to address the process of how we learn to compose (or improvise) our lives—both in and out of schools. The musician and poet, teacher and researcher in me is interested in the un/familiar refrain that draws together those of us interested in this kind of dance, one that is not only pedagogical but also epistemological and methodological—and artistic. I'm referring to the creative process itself, in which there is some grand combination of desire, frustration, mystery, imagination, passion, intention, joy, humor, light, tension, darkness, improvisation, attention, humor—and above all—a willingness to suspend knowing. Another way of stating this last characteristic might be to describe the process as an embrace of not-knowing on the way (perhaps) to knowing.

So, yes, on any given Thursday afternoon, we are likely to find ourselves involved in some kind of improvisational activity set within a musical and/or dramatic context. The children seem to speak this un-language with relative ease. We might be sitting in a circle passing a (musical) note around, experimenting with pitch or tone. Five minutes later, we might find ourselves fully engaged in a "play" in which we are all animals of the forest moving about in search of food. The (multiple) roles I have chosen for myself (and perhaps these roles have also chosen me) as well as the multiple roles I invite the children to try on are themselves improvised in ways that require both them and me to embrace uncertainty.

Improvisation, this making something from nothing, is itself musical and playful. As a teacher and researcher, improvisation troubles my practice, it fascinates me, disturbs me, provokes me. Improvisation chases me, chooses me: it is the place I find myself returning to, again and again, it's where the energy is—this place of imagination and risk, pleasure and surprise. It doesn't seem to matter whether I'm talking about teaching or learning, writing or making music. Or researching. Improvisation threads its way through all I do. So, what can we learn about learning from improvisation? Can we learn to repeat an essentially unrepeatable act? Can we learn to live well with the (apparent) contradiction and paradox of practicing improvisation?

Questions about improvisation (and composition) also become questions of pedagogy and research: How do we create/improvise a song/life of our own? How do we improvise/create a song with others? How do we help others sing their songs? How do we learn to bring our voices to the singing? How do we help others with their voices without our own voices becoming too loud? How do we learn to make music together in *every* kind of classroom? And finally, how do we learn to create/improvise the conditions required to live creatively with these kinds of questions? What might research "look like" as an improvisational act that seeks to spend time with people, as Mary Catherine Bateson would have it, "engaged in the act of creation that engages us all—the composition of our lives" (1989, p. 1).

I'm the butterfly now. You sing when my wings move. . . .

These are Jennifer's words; they tumbled out one afternoon during a memorable "improv" session together. These kinds of beautiful gems emerge, uncut and sparkling, from the mouths of the children every time we're together. This constant waterfall of words, steeped in wisdom, that pours forth from kids is no surprise to anyone who works and plays with children. But how to capture it all? All this data. And what to do with the words and music and sounds as they flow and flow and flow without end? How do I manage to re-present the spirit of improvisation without bringing the performance to a standstill? How do I juggle *this* role, my role as data dancer?

If it were not a process, there would be no surprise. . . .

Part 2, Imagine, Inventing a Data-dancer (A Poem)

Dancing Data: Scenario 11.8b (January, 2001)

Track 1: Jennifer talks about her creative process, her wild and untested theory of songmaking . . . .
Track 2: A musical excerpt from one of our musicmaking sessions
Track 3: A collage of children's voices wrestling happily with an improvisation piece
Track 4: Jennifer's teacher speaking "live" as she listens and responds to Jennifer's song
Track 5: My voice describing one particular scenario in which Jennifer emerges as a butterfly to orchestrate and direct her friends in an improvisation session
Track 6: My voice reading a passage from my own writing of this chapter and dancing the data
Track 7: A poetic voice reading a Maxine Greene passage from *Releasing the Imagincation*
Track 8: A poetic voice reading the Grade Two Music Curriculum document

To make a short story long, I decided to go out and buy an expensive machine in order to help me dance the data. [Not that money—or technology—can buy researcherly satisfaction.]

This new piece of technology—this toy I purchased—gathers voices up and stores them in multifarious and complex ways. I believe it's going to help me honor the cacophony of the human utterance where meaning surfaces and then dives down deeper.

I've decided to call this machine
a data-dancer, it dances
data in ways that make me
epistemologically dizzy. Data will never
be the same   again.

The data-dancer makes theory
practice. It resists
any kind of closure and insists
on the interminability of the data its dances.

There will be happy collisions and lack of precision.

The data-dancer (makes) practice(s)
theory. It does not work without help. I have also

purchased a (very) good microphone—one that hears
everything and approximates nothing
we are used to hearing. (It, too, was expensive.)

As costly as it may have been, the data-dancer can't think
on its own. It simply records and stores and manipulates
digital data in as many ways as I can imagine.

This multi-tracking machine is simply a re-presenter. It
helps me live in the hyphenated space of re-presentation.
It reminds me that all I am doing
is manipulating (dancing)   data.

It is a processor that assists me in honouring
process. It is a purposeful confounder.
It mixes, melds, matches, melts, mangles
dumps, dangles, downloads and even disses data.

The data-dancer is a precision
blender, a juxtapositioner that
causes effects—it distorts, delays, amplifies, reverberates,
  and, given short
notice, can become a   chorus.

I know what you're thinking: the
data-dancer is delusional, it's just
another (expensive) gimmick.   And you may be right. . . .]

How will the data-dancer help me
get to the heart of things? I don't know.   [Yet . . .]

What will I do
with the data-
dancer?   [I can only imagine. . . .]

The data-dancer is a Yamaha MD8 (Multitrack MiniDisc Recording Unit). The microphone is a Rode NT1. They're beautiful objects in their own right, though I can't believe I'm saying this. I used to love to hate technology. But here I am (and are these dials and buttons ever cool. . . .) I'm still not sure how to work this machine but the

Owner's Manual is 106 pages long and I have generous friends who really *do* know what they're doing.

It's not all that difficult to bring the dancer with me when I visit the school and, believe it or not, there aren't that many wires or cords to deal with. Oh yes, and there isn't any kind of recording tape, just these neat and tidy little discs. . . .

How seriously shall we take ourselves?

Keep in the mind that the data-dancer is always ready to re-present the re-presentation at any given moment. Each and every track can be altered, played with, so that any particular track can be brought up or down (made more prominent or alternately buried) in the mix. Effects can be added that create any number of possible results. A voice can be distorted or delayed so that it begins to perform itself, differently. Tracks can be introduced at staggered times in order to build soundscapes that create different moods and feelings. These combinations and permutations are neither good nor bad, just *different*. . . .

What to do with all of this data?

But there is *so* much data to dance. (And this is not necessarily a good thing.) The sound bytes can overwhelm. Everything wants to be data. This is the danger. This is the drug. I don't necessarily want to be in charge of all of this data. (In fact, I may need professional help.) I suppose I could seek funding in order to hire technicians to spin the dials and set up the microphones and sort the sound files. I could also invite the kids to help work with the dancer. And I will. I will most certainly invite them to mix and re-mix the stuff we record together. It's not mine, this data, though it's always tempting to lay claim. It's too easy to play puppeteer and pull the strings in order to make the data dance in ways that best suit *me*. . . .

Part 3, Dancing the Data

What would it mean to truly confound, conflate, confuse, collude,
[What are we doing this for?] [You told us last week we were going
construct, collate, and otherwise compose the data in various ways
to use the microphone today!] [Kevin, can you please leave the
of our own choosing? What would it mean to add the elements of
equipment alone and come back and join us, here? We need your at-
collision and collusion to this growing list of c-words as we employ

tention.] [Do we miss recess because of this?] [O.K., so what
the data-dancer to purposefully dance the data, purposefully
we're trying to do here today is to get each of you to read a new
create soundscapes that both lead and mis-lead? What if, in addi-
script I've made for you—Jennifer, can I have your attention here
tion to simply altering the nature of how some of the data recorded
please? It's too distracting telling everyone what's going on with
with the kids is re-presented, we "changed" the data, altogether?
you talking to Sasha.] [What do I do with this data now . . .?]

Purposefully fictionalized the data? Faked the data, even? What if Jennifer, Sasha, Brant, Kelly, Kevin, Julia, and Robyn were to become someone other than themselves? (Someone other?) What if, for example, a group of teachers became the voices of Jennifer and company in Scenario 11.8b (previously described)? How might our relationship with the data—and the nature of the research project—change? What if we were to change the nature of the scenario itself, so that Jennifer, Sasha and company are no longer the wonderful group of children that I first described them as? (See the "bold" font above.)

When is this kind of manipulation of data simply manipulative? At what point is the trust between researcher and participant, researcher and reader, betrayed? When does play push meaning aside and confirm the critics of postmodernism's most pointed concerns?

> Dancing the Data, Scenario 11.9d (March 2001)
> *Track 1:* Julia's voice is heard above those of her classmates; these are the sounds of a thriving and creative group of kids working together.
> *Track 2:* A drum loop builds, gradually offering a familiar yet somehow unsteadying influence as the scenario unfolds.
> *Track 3:* A quirky melody is introduced, performed on a xylophone, invoking the elementary school music room (the ones that *used* to exist before we decided to get "back to the basics"). This melody begins to draw attention to itself as it bends and twists to create an almost imperceptible undercurrent of tension.
> *Track 4:* Kevin's voice emerges as he succeeds in creating one distraction after another—anything to draw attention away from the project and on to himself.

Dancing the Data, Scenario 11.9d (The "Ugly Scenario")
Jennifer. Sasha. Brant. Kelly. Kevin. Julia. Robyn. Seven children: seven reasons why many teachers fear exploring music with their students. A curricular nightmare in the making. We never quite get around

> This sucks . . . .

to making music. Too little time, too many arguments. Brant appears

Track 5: A second instrument is introduced. A recorder, another instrument used widely in elementary schools at one time, begins to create a melodic interplay with the xylophone. This has the effect of further unsettling the re-presentation. [Narrator's voice rises & fades, rises & fades.]
Track 6: A conversation unfolds between three successful and innovative high school music teachers. As their conversation progresses, each voice doubles up on itself, producing a pronounced "fattening" effect.
Track 7: Jennifer's voice is "stuck" on a kind of repeat, an endless loop that spills out one phrase.
Track 8: My voice offers self-reflexive insights on this particular research scene.

appears to take great pleasure in ensuring that Jennifer and Julia know that their ideas are stupid. Sasha wants to make a video (with her as star). Kevin can't stop messing with the (very expensive) recording equipment I drag to their classroom each week. . . .

So why the data-dancer? As I continue to live with the notion of dancing the data (and the realization that we are always and already dancing the data no matter what conscious and unconscious decisions we may make with the research that we are learning to live with in our lives), I have become more and more fascinated with the concept of *purposefully playing with data,* more and more at home with the conviction that data must, indeed, be danced (as opposed to tamed or quieted or ordered). Why? For a host of reasons that seem to dissolve in solution with one another when it comes time to identify and articulate them.

First, I believe that playing with data *is* a form of (research) work. Yes, play is a form of work. Play can be the working of form (playfully), while work can be a playing with form. Whether it takes place through poetry or imaginative wordplay, through improvisation or through a deliberate and patient combination of planning and dreaming and waiting—I'm thinking of Uncle Jim in his winter shack—research is, above all, a process.

I believe process is more important than outcome. It's certainly more interesting to me. Internationally renowned graphic designer Bruce Mau says that "when the outcome drives the process we will only ever go to where we've already been. If process drives outcome we may not know where we're going, but we will know we want to be there" (1999, p. 56).

It will come as no surprise that I believe research is an imaginative act. As I give myself permission to follow my passions and my instincts, however quirky they might initially seem, I find myself paying attention to the places and spaces where the imagination casts its own lovely light upon research. I am more concerned with letting go of the literal rather than documenting it. There needs to be more room to imagine what might have taken place as we dwell with our research, more time to imagine what *might* take place given the power to imagine. Using the data-dancer to dance data into previously unimagined combinations and permutations makes surprise a constant possibility. What we think we know (or don't know) can be made available to us in new and unexpected ways. Surprise and detour, in this way, become important elements that help shape meaning and affect the ways we relate to our data.

Although it has taken on unhelpful baggage, curricular and otherwise, imagination is not a lightweight word. John Dewey paints imagination as "the large and generous blending of interests at the point where the mind comes in contact with the world. When old and familiar things are made new in experience, there is imagination" (1934, p. 267). I feel strongly that we must risk the imaginative in our work, risk the ways that imagination might make our research appear less real, less valued by some. In fact, there must be room for all of our voices, less hurry to find fault in one another's process. Imagine that. . . .

So dancing the data is, for me, simply another way to make more explicit the play that is already there, seeking ritualization and exploration rather than resolution. Ritualization and exploration rather than resolution. . . .

And, finally, the data-dancer, with its ability to purposefully confound data, encourages self-reflexivity, a research strategy and life practice that can assist us in addressing those things that trouble our practice. As artists and researchers, self-reflexivity enables us to point to ourselves pointing to the world while pointing out the risks and richness, the foibles and the fallibility, of our enterprises as we go. Self-reflexivity can bring earnestness and irony together to bear upon one another and inform our practice, provide it with depth and levity. Self-reflexivity is the hinge of problem/opportunity upon which much of my work rests, it enables me to continue processing my process as I go; it implicates me in whatever story I choose to tell, whatever data I might attempt to dance.

Can we imagine data that dances?

Notes

1. Pseudonyms are used throughout the chapter with reference to the Grade 3 students.

2. In a somewhat disconcerting sense I have become the music teacher for the school. Why? Because we live in a (dangerous) time when government directives steer schools toward so-called "accountability," leaving many programs, like music, open to the ever-present and ongoing budget crises which threaten to dismantle the very things that run through the heart and soul of schools.

References

Bateson, M. C. (1989). *Composing a life.* New York: Penguin.

Bateson, M. C. (1994). *Peripheral visions: Learning along the way.* New York: Harper/Collins.

Dewey, J. (1934). *Art as experience.* New York: Perigee Books.

Greene, M. (1995). *Releasing the imagination: Essays on education, the arts and social change.* San Francisco: Jossey-Bass.

Leggo, C. (1999). *View from my mother's house.* St. John's, Newfoundland, Canada: Killick Press.

Mau, B. (1999, March/April). An incomplete manifesto for growth. *I.D. Magazine,* 56–58.

Richardson, L. (1994). Writing: A method of inquiry. In N. Denzin & Y. Lincoln (Eds.), *Handbook of qualitative research* (pp. 516–529). Thousand Oaks, CA: Sage.

Sumara, D. (1996). Using commonplace books in curriculum studies. *Journal of Curriculum Theorizing, 12*(1), 45–48.

Winterson, J. (1996). *Art objects: Essays on ecstasy and effrontery.* London: Vintage.

PART THREE

Visual Arts Data

CHAPTER 8

Artistry, Inquiry, and Sense-of-Place: Secondary School Students Portrayed in Context

J. GARY KNOWLES AND SUZANNE M. THOMAS

On a warm, humid, summer day, Gary stepped into the Art Gallery at Carleton University, Ottawa, Canada, and discovered a retrospective exhibit of photographic installations entitled *Landworks 1979–1991* by Marlene Creates, an internationally renowned photographer from Newfoundland, Canada. In this serendipitous moment he experienced a strong, responsive resonance with the artist's work. As a practicing artist and researcher, Gary felt a growing need to fuse artistry into scholarly production (see Finley & Knowles, 1995) and knew intuitively that the processes, perspectives, and representational elements evident in Marlene Creates' work were analogous to the methodological basis of his own life history research:

> Key components of life history inquiry were visibly present [in the retrospective exhibit]: exploration of a life through recounting memories of experiences and the meanings attributed to them; evidence of substantial effort over time given to obtaining the stories of a life; contextualization of a life lived; and, representation of a life which honored the individual, celebrating life, yet raising to consciousness important understandings about the value of the life and its relation to larger questions of society. (Cole & Knowles, 2001, pp. 59–60)

The account that follows is one that renders elements of our experiences as they are sparked and creatively inspired by Marlene

Creates' work. We are enticed by the power of visual art processes and forms to infuse more organic, holistic processes into researching endeavors. Art that is fused and embedded into the processes and representations of social science research comes to inform and enrich our inquiry in synergistic and arresting ways.

Our project, *Fusing Artistry into Scholarship, Students Portrayed in Context,* involves secondary school art students in an exploration of *place* and *sense-of-place* in school and interweaves the elements and perspectives of Marlene Creates' artistry into life history-like researching processes. This orientation does not seeks to infringe upon the creativity of Marlene Creates and the uniqueness of her work but, rather, reflects learning from, and responsiveness to, the discipline of art as a way of informing alternative information gathering and representational modes of social science and educational inquiry.

We enter into this inquiry as two artist-researcher-educators intent on challenging conventions and pushing the boundaries of traditional scholarship. We want to expand the processes and representations of life history research by moving from the tape recorder and transcriber to the camera and paintbrush; from the computer to the art-making studio; from talking to small, specialized audiences to engaging with larger communities; from the halls of the academy to the walls of an art gallery.

We come to this researching endeavor as artists: Gary as a visual artist typically working with water media paints on paper and canvas, Suzanne with an interest in poetry, printmaking, and photography; as educators, Gary with twelve years of secondary school teaching experience designing innovative outdoor, experiential education programs and continuing that work with preservice teachers and graduate students at universities, Suzanne with eight years experience developing interdisciplinary literary and visual arts programs in elementary schools as well as work with preservice teachers in university contexts. As researchers with nontraditional perspectives, we share a compelling desire to re-envision what it means to conduct research and to engage in scholarly production. Our personal worldviews reflect a need to represent, with authenticity, the multidimensionalities and complexities of human lives. We hold a strong commitment to extend the realm of academic discourse by locating it in a public forum and making it accessible to wider audiences. These are but some of the fundamental assumptions, understandings, and guiding principles that emanate from the heart of our work.

We locate this inquiry within the emerging genre of educational research referred to as arts-informed inquiry (see Cole & Knowles, 2000, 2001; Finley & Knowles, 1995; Watrin, 1999). So it is that we draw inspiration from the artistic enterprise and creativity of Marlene Creates and focus on the translation of her work and processes into an inquiry form (see Knowles & Thomas, 2001, for another articulation of this aspect of our work). Central to the conceptualization of our inquiry, then, is the fusion of an artist's inquiry methods, elements, and theoretical perspectives that provides a multidimensional framework for the generation of, at once, data or information *and* representational forms. This is what makes our work arts-informed—the processes of artistry are infused into the life-blood of our efforts like an elixir bolsters the body's health and well-being.

Marlene Creates' photography is highly evocative—it is charged with the meanings associated with humans-in-context, of people located-in-place. It depicts lives-in-context (the hallmark characteristic of life history research) and provides an aesthetically creative, visual and textual representation of lives lived. Marlene's model of inquiry and representation consists of assemblages in which she explores the relationships between human experience and landscape, nature and culture, and sense-of-place. Marlene is a "quintessential phenomenologist" whose art reflects "a condition of acute receptivity—a kind of porousness—in which she opens herself to a place . . . and then responds to what the site suggests to her" (Garvey, 1993, p. 1). She states that her purpose in exploring the natural, physical world is not to see the most spectacular landscape but, rather, to "see what is there" and to get a feel for the "spirit of the place" (Creates, 1994).

> The kind of terrain that draws me is open topographies like the moorlands, the arctic tundra, the prairies and the plains, the desert and the sea. My works are not so much about these environments, though, but about our human relationship with them, including the way urban environments have been affected by their geographical location. . . . I am interested in the intersections between experience, memory, language, and the land. . . . Most of my work is in the form of photo-based assemblages and installations, often combining text and found objects with the photographic image. . . . My works are not answers, they are questions. These questions have to do with the complexities of our relationship to the physical world. (Creates, 1997)

In our project with students, Marlene Creates provides the conceptual framework for information gathering, artifact collection, and the transformation of data into multi-modal, representational forms. We especially take inspiration from works depicted in her retrospective exhibit, *Places of Presence: Newfoundland Kin and Ancestral Land, Newfoundland 1989–1991* and in *The Distance between Two Points Is Measured in Memories, Labrador 1988*. In *Places of Presence* she endeavors to capture through the camera's lens, in stark black and white photographs, the raw feelings and persona of her distant, elderly relatives. She gathers information and artifacts about *their* sense-of-place through a collection of images, stories, and drawings of cognitive memory maps that depict vivid memories of place experience within rugged, barren, bleak landscapes along the northeastern shores of North America. These are evocative works that unfold within intimate spaces.

We were initially drawn to infuse Marlene Creates' vision of life history explorations due to our resonance with the processes and forms of her work—yet we have another motivating goal. We are aware of the paucity of authentic portrayals of students' contemporary, lived experiences of school within educational research and are moved to capture youthful experiences and perspectives through Creates-like explorations of sense-of-place. In the midst of current political upheaval in schools in Ontario, Canada, for example—work-to-rule actions by teachers, changes in the Ontario Curriculum, implementation of standardized testing, massive school board amalgamations, increased class sizes, reduced emphasis on the arts, and elimination of extracurricular programs—we want to understand the raw social realities of students' engagement or disengagement in secondary schools. We wonder for example: Do students feel a strong identification with their school? Do they experience a sense of school spirit, sense-of-place, or sense of community? What are the relations between students within school, students and teachers, students and community? What do students view as school-wide issues amid the crisis of Ontario public education?

Given these questions, the purpose of our inquiry was to examine secondary school art students' sense-of-place, locatedness, or placelessness within their educative contexts. We wanted to gain insight from students who come from a diversity of political, social, economic, and familial backgrounds, to engage them as prime collectors, articulators, and interpreters of experience by enabling them to assume full control over their individual inquiry process. This approach is significant since little educational research directly involves students in the gathering, arranging, analyzing, or representing of information related to schools, curriculum, or pedagogy from their perspectives (see Erickson & Shultz, 1992; Pollard, Thiessen, & Filer, 1997). We are interested in presenting, for both public display and scholarly interrogation and analysis, visual and artistic images *of* and *by* students—accomplished within the context of their classrooms and schools—that depict their varied experiences of place in multiple and authentic ways.

We involved the students in an exploration of *place* not only to gain an understanding of their contemporary lived experiences of school but to get a sense of those acquired over a lifetime. We defined *place* as an individual and socially constructed reality (Hutchison, 1999; Relph, 1976)—a notion that integrates elements of geographical location, social consciousness, and the meanings derived from experience-in-place. Broadly, for the purposes of this work, we regard place as a physical location within school (or school property) that, for an individual, epitomizes or characterizes specific emotional experiences associated with being a student in school at this specific point in time, location, and history. It is a place that represents, in literal or metaphorical terms, a focusing of a student's emotive response to the "sociophysical" context of school (Berleant, 1997).

Marlene Creates' artistry, its structure and transparent processes, was reinterpreted and modified for the purposes of the students' inquiries. We asked the senior secondary school students, those taking photography and visual arts courses, to create an authentic portrayal of their special or significant place at school by responding to requests such as these: Tell us about your experiences of school. Tell us about your place in school. Tell us about a significant place within or immediately outside the school building. Convey to us how you see yourself in this place. Tell us what you think about school as a place to be. We then asked them to apply a model or structure to their inquiry and artistry based on Marlene's photographic life history investigations. This inquiry model framework includes seven linked elements providing students with a multidimensional and multi-modal representation format: self-portrait, memory map, photo of place, narrative, photo of self-in-place, found object, and a two-or three-dimensional artwork. With our assistance, and that of their art teachers, the students conceptualized and developed their artistry.

On completion of the students' depictions of experience-in-place, we assumed the task of uncovering the essential messages inherent in their work. Conscious of our researcher roles, we viewed the artwork as educators familiar with schools and, at the same time, as practicing artists. We made visual and contextual interpretations of the photographic images, the narratives, and the other elements of the students' work (see Becker, 1998; Davey, 1999; Harper, 1994, 1998). We examined the multi-framed assemblages—taking note of our emotive response and intuitive understandings—with an openness to the individual and collective voices of student-artists. By immersing ourselves in their art, we focused on the depictions of place and the feelings evoked; the drama, mood, and tone of the images; the interrelatedness and coherence of the images with the text; the emphasis given to *place* and theme in the work as a whole; the balance and composition of the images; and the relationship between the images, text, and maps. This is our "dancing with the data"—an evocative, responsive task. This is the context for the intersection of heart and mind, artist and viewer, teacher and student, researcher and individual.

We listened to the voices of imagery (Prosser & Schwartz, 1998) and interrogated students' artwork for understandings of their individual and collective life history experiences of school. We asked questions of the representations themselves, attempting to explore the meanings of the works, in a way that is similar to the response of an art viewer at a professional artist's exhibition—an example of lives intersecting for mutual meaning-making (Denzin, 1998). New meanings are always derived as the viewer/reader's life intersects with that of the artist. With "imaginative empathy" and "sensitive engagement" (Whiteley, 1999, p. 117), rather than a spirit of artistic connoisseurship (Barone & Eisner, 1997), we combined insight and thoughtful interpretations of the students' images with the full range of our own experiences of art produced within communities and for social, political, and cultural purposes. The ideas and questions we derived from these viewings and our heartfelt responses to students' work formed the basis for dialogues with student-artists. Through these conversations we gained insight into their inquiry processes and the fundamental conceptualization of their artwork in order to understand more about the relationship of the represented experience to other experiences of school. In doing this we assisted students in crafting artist statements outlining the underlying intentions, emotions, and processes of the displayed artistry.

Our responses to the artwork, in addition to conversations with students and consultation with their teachers, allowed us to transform the artistic artifacts/information (Wolcott, 1994). The students revealed their challenges, struggles, insights, and new perspectives gained through their artistic sense-of-place explorations. Points of resonance emerged and connections began to unfold as they retrospectively uncovered the processes of their inquiry experiences. They articulated an understanding of place as "seen from the inside" (Lippard, 1997) and a developing awareness of the connection between interior and exterior landscapes, self and place, self and world. In searching to find *place,* one student reveals, "You need to find a place within yourself first before you can represent sense-of-place." Many of the students indicate that the *place* they chose to represent "reflects their inner selves" and they express a commonality of emotions that encompass feelings of isolation, a sense of vulnerability, and a need for a sense of belonging in school. These feelings were made known through their artistry and in their words. For example, here is Heather's[1] description:

> It is in this place that I feel most VULNERABLE. In a sense of awkwardness I disappear and reappear to the delight of some. As I return, I find things impossibly like the way I left them, surreal-like in a world fathomed by immune nature. Through this I have discovered something. A rebirth if I may call it, of all that is just true and just in my life. A push from a force awakening me to a different vision, one of liberation and an abounding passion. I have delivered my greatest moments to an audience of image and now bask in the fake admiration of numbers. I do not look back; for I fear I will return to stone, or be smothered by insecurity. I press on in fight that seems like a battle against the world, and find myself exuding exhaustion with a smile. This push has been the demise of my very existence, but has proved enlightening, for I have found the one thing everyone searches for, MYSELF.

Students raised issues of identity by referring to their self-portraits. "I am not really seen in my self-portrait." "I feel that I am not noticed at school." "I do not look into the camera lens because I don't let people see me at school. I am scared of being criticized." Other responses included the following: "My portrait is cropped closely around my face to represent the lack of freedom I feel at school." "I double-exposed the portrait of me in the foreground to emphasize how my place in school is vague and uncertain."

Schools are viewed by these students as large, monolithic structures that constrain freedom—impersonal institutions that no longer promote community spirit, encourage sense-of-place, or provide them with a sense of community (Sanger, 1997). "I struggle to find my place. Finding my place is difficult because we don't have a community at school. We don't have a chance to belong in school with friends and to relax without worries." Another student comments, reflecting on the changing curricular context, "We no longer have clubs, social events, extra-curricular activities and our community spirit is disappearing."

As students engaged in their "dance with the data" they heard echoing sounds and reverberations as their images spoke in polyphonic voices. One student declared that "Photography reveals the photographer. The nature of photography, as with many arts, is a form of expression when words are insufficient." The medium of photography allowed students to make statements perhaps more difficult to convey in words—their images became "social constructions" in-context (Becker, 1998, p. 84) and the world we viewed as an audience was "saturated with sociological meaning" (Harper, 1998, p. 38). Students uncovered in their photo-based assemblages a sense of solitude, a sense of aloneness, feelings of vulnerability, and a growing sense of placelessness. They identified, for themselves, the fact that many of the places depicted through their photo-based installations represented solitary places for quiet reflection.

The Darkroom: Where Two Solitudes Meet

A ROOM.
Set back and above the buzzing school
Is a space of peace,
The quiet mind of this institute.

It is a room filled with darkness.
People enter timid and cautious.
But intimidation becomes security.
To know a place well that is devoid of light is a comfort.

My eyes adjust and blindness turns to illumination.
Opposites unite as black on my negative
Keeps my paper white.

THE DARK.
I have found myself here many times.
It is a hiding place,
A mask that I wear.

The darkness is accepted ignorance,
A cleared mind.
And through it comes an image,
A reflection of reality.
And Outside the people may recognize my perception.

Outside, the light assumes knowledge.
The light casts shadows.
I take the security and identity of the darkroom
Of being alone.
I take it Outside.
Just as we sleep in the dark
And carry our renewal through the day,
I carry the strength of solitude that I met in the darkroom.
(Amelia Single-Kat)

Marlene Creates traveled from Newfoundland to Ontario to attend the Opening Exhibit of the student artwork at a Toronto art gallery. The exhibition also included one of her assemblages, "Gilbert Rich, Labrador, 1988," from the series *The Distance between Two Points Is Measured in Memories*. We observed Marlene standing humbly before students' work, viewing it, feeling it, deeply moved by the emotive and evocative nature of the students' photographs, drawings, memory maps, images, and words. She, too, "danced with the data" by immersing herself fully in their artwork and narrative texts. She was honored that her work sparked artistic explorations, produced creative responses, and provoked introspective thought. We, along with Marlene, regarded the collective exhibit as a forum for communication and interaction. We witnessed the power of multiple representations to become a complex language and visual dialogue that empowered students by giving voice to their experience.

The exhibit extended the collective inquiry beyond an academic setting to inform the community at large of the social conditions of schools and of students' experiences within institutional educative contexts. Students noted the diversity of their representational forms as well as their appreciation of the opportunity to exhibit their work publicly alongside that of an internationally renowned Canadian artist. They were honored that others valued their work as artists and acknowledged the place of art in learning and society.

Our experiences reinforce the notion that the contributions of the arts to processes of and forms for representing research are particularly promising for sifting out understandings of the complex interaction between individual lives lived within organizational and institutional contexts. Just as contemporary artist Martha Rosler considers the responsibility of the artist to society in *Place, Position, Power, Politics,* we pose this same question in relation to the academy and ask what is the role and responsibility of the researcher to society? In doing so, we challenge ourselves to cease the perpetual "walling off of intellectual activity in institutions" (Rosler, 1994, p. 61) by assuming the task of seeking public exhibition space, and to face the continuing dilemma of determining how to reach wider audiences effectively. Our goal is to provide exhibition forums that will achieve this, to inform conventional knowledge about students' experiences of school, and to pose insightful questions about schools as primary sites of adolescents' educational learning.

We envision that arts-informed depictions of human experience, seen through the lens of visual artist-researchers, may enrich the complex rendering of stories and personal histories in ways that are multi-textural, multi-layered, and multidimensional. The raw realities of many unheard students' lives, depicted by the emotive nature of their two-and three-dimensional artwork, allowed students to reveal school experiences in ways that were of their own construction.

We strive to reach beyond the academic, institutional context to inform educational policymakers, curriculum developers, school boards, administrators, educators, and the public at large of the social conditions of schools. We will continue to explore the cultural dynamics of individual students in educative contexts and identify the qualities and dimensions of *place* that are most influential in shaping the ways students approach learning. We believe in the empowerment of students by engaging them in constructing youth-generated knowledge of *sense-of-place* and by providing them with opportunities to inform the general public of social and educational implications that may lead to questioning the status quo in schools and, eventually, bring about school improvement.

We see the potential for artists' processes and perspectives to greatly enliven and inform scholarly work. We see them enhancing researchers' conceptualizations of inquiry processes and methodological designs. We see them increasing understandings of art as a way of knowing the self and exploring the world. This arts-informed research approach is unique in the extent to which the convention and form of art influences the inquiry process and inquiry product, just as the multidimensional exhibit of student artwork represents, simultaneously, the elements of a multifaceted information gathering process as well as the production of meaning-making and knowledge.

Apart from our motivations for involving students our intent in applying the constructs derived from Marlene Creates' work was to infuse more organic processes into our research endeavors, to embed our work in processes that honor our own unique perspectives of the world, and to extend the potential for scholarship to communicate with the community beyond the academy. Marlene Creates' work has informed our authentic and innovative engagement in life history educational research—she as artist played the music that inspired us to dance.

Notes

1. All names are pseudonyms.

References

Barone, T. E., & Eisner, E. (1997). Arts-based educational research. In R. M. Jaegar (Ed.), *Complementary methods for research in education* (pp. 73–116). Washington, DC: American Educational Research Association.

Becker, S. (1998). Visual sociology, documentary photography and photo-journalism: It's (almost) all a matter of context. In J. Prosser (Ed.), *Image-based research: A sourcebook for qualitative researchers* (pp. 84–96). London: Falmer Press.

Berleant, A. (1997). *Living in the landscape.* Kansas City: University Press of Kansas.

Cole, A. L., & Knowles, J. G. (2000). *Researching teaching: Exploring teacher development through reflexive inquiry.* New York: Allyn & Bacon.

Cole, A. L., & Knowles, J. G. (2001). *Lives in context: The art of life history research.* Walnut Creek, CA: AltaMira Press.

Creates, M. (1990). *The distance between two points is measured in memories, Labrador 1998.* North Vancouver, British Columbia, Canada: Presentation House Gallery.

Creates, M. (1991). *Places of presence: Newfoundland kin and ancestral land, Newfoundland 1989–1991.* St. John's, Newfoundland, Canada: Killick Press.

Creates, M. (1992). *Marlene Creates: Landworks 1979–1991* (S. Gibson Garvey, Ed. and Curator) St. John's, Newfoundland, Canada: Memorial University of Newfoundland.

Creates, M. (1994). *A hand to standing stones, Scotland 1983.* Artist statement.

Creates, M. (1997). Untitled artist statement.

Davey, N. (1999). The hermeneutics of seeing. In I. Heywood & B. Sandywell (Eds.),

Interpreting visual culture: Explorations in the hermeneutics of the visual (pp. 3–29). London: Routledge.

Denzin, N. K. (1998). The art and politics of interpretation. In N. K. Denzin & Y. S. Lincoln (Eds.), *Collecting and interpreting qualitative materials* (pp. 313–344). Thousand Oaks, CA: Sage.

Erickson, F., & Shultz, J. (1992). *Handbook of Research on Curriculum*, New York: Macmillan.

Finley, S., & Knowles, J. G. (1995). Researcher as artist/Artist as researcher. *Qualitative Inquiry, 1*(1), 110–142.

Garvey, S. G. (Ed. & Curator), (1993). *Marlene Creates: Landworks 1979–1991*. St. John's, Newfoundland: Memorial University of Newfoundland.

Harper, D. (1994). On the authority of the image: Visual methods at the crossroads. In N. K. Denzin & Y. S. Lincoln (Eds.), *Collecting and interpreting qualitative materials* (pp.130–149). Thousand Oaks, CA: Sage.

Harper, D. (1998). An argument for visual sociology. In J. Prosser (Ed.), *Image-based research: A sourcebook for qualitative researchers* (pp. 24–41). London: Falmer Press.

Hutchison, D. (1999). *Perspectives on place in education*. Unpublished doctoral thesis, Ontario Institute for Studies in Education of the University of Toronto, Toronto, Ontario, Canada.

Knowles, J. G., & Thomas, S. (2001). Insights and inspiration from an artist's work: Envisioning and portraying lives-in-context. In A. L. Cole & J. G. Knowles, *Lives-in-context: The art of life history research* (pp. 208–214). Walnut Creek, CA: AltaMira Press.

Lippard, L. (1997). *The lure of the local: Senses of place in a multi-centered society.* New York: The New Press.

Pollard, A., Thiessen, D., & Filer, A. (Eds.). (1997). *Children and their curriculum: The perspectives of primary and elementary school children.* London: Falmer Press.

Prosser, J., & Schwartz, D. (1998). Photographs within the sociological research process. In J. Prosser (Ed.), *Image-based research: A sourcebook for qualitative researchers* (pp. 115–130). London: Falmer Press.

Relph, E. (1976). *Place and placelessness*. London: Pion Ltd.

Rosler, M. (1994). Place, position, power, politics. In C. Becker (Ed.), *The subversive imagination: Artists, society, and social responsibility* (pp. 55–76). London: Routledge.

Sanger, M. (1997). Sense of place in education. *The Journal of Environmental Education, 29*(1), 4–8.

Watrin, R. (1999). Art as research. *Canadian Review of Art Education, 26*(2), 92–100.

Whiteley, N. (1999). Readers of the lost art: Visuality and particularity in art criticism. In I. Heywood & B. Sandywell (Eds.), *Interpreting visual culture: Explorations in the hermeneutics of the visual* (pp. 99–122). London: Routledge.

Wolcott, H. F. (1994). *Transforming qualitative data: Description, analysis, and interpretation*. Thousand Oaks, CA: Sage.

CHAPTER 9

Showcasing Arts-Based Inquiries

CAROL A. MULLEN = C. T. PATRICK DIAMOND[1]

Dancing on the wing, for sheer joy played
And sang, like images took flight
—Heaney, *Death of a Naturalist*

Carnival Barker as a Postmodern Leader-Promoter

Step right up! Time to sing and dance! Carnival visitors just show your entry ticket to find your place at your designated table and introduce yourself to your troupe: The Illusionists, The Trapeze Fliers, The Jugglers, The Tight-Rope Walkers, The Tumbling Acrobats, The Untamed Animals, and The Fire-Eaters!

Put down that journal! Imagine the public educational researcher as a carnival/circus barker. To evoke the revelry of Postmodern Arts-Based Educational Research (PABER), we release in this chapter the words and acts of others who were co-participants in our most recent circus performance. We lead here too as in a dance but only to suggest a promising arrangement of steps, a way forward, and a way of orchestrating a joint performance. Here, and in a recent show for which we acted as mistress/master of ceremonies (Mullen & Diamond, 2001), we use carnival as a transgressive metaphor for educational research conducted as entertainment and diversion. We risk situating ourselves differently as multi-tasked educational researchers who function as choreographer-publicizer-barkers. Standing before the entrance to the funfair/showground, we solicit you, our customers, with our larger than life colorful spiel (the rationale). Let us entice you into a new research relationship that joins barker and audience/performer. We will conduct you on a dis/organized tour of the different acts (the data) that we describe and comment on (the analysis). But you had better watch your step! We too may be promising more than can be delivered. With this disclaimer, however, we hope to problematize/subvert the exalted reform promises of those opinion leaders who, as if campaigning for political office, offer the "quick fix" with the all too glib assurance of test scores forever rising.

As joint carnival barker-spokespersons, we expound and advocate for arts-based forms of inquiry and on behalf of artist researchers. Using arts-based forms to defy the comfortable and simplistic modernist notions of what *counts* in educational research, we seek performances that take the form of wire dancing with free expression and movement. We offer postmodernist arts-based inquiry as a way to lose our cool! Even as we have set out to do here, "it's time for the show to go on!" and for us to dare a possible fall—to feel and evoke that sinking sensation as an opportunity for inciting new forms of engagement, community, and arts-based inquiry. The barker helps others to see possibilities and to free themselves.

Although the barker is found in many guises, we present the barker as an idealistic figure, the "emissary-prophet" (Weber, 1919/1946), but only in the sense of soliciting the wondrous insights of others. As a critical as well as a prophetic leader, the barker encourages the questioning of and the rebellion against all conventional/complacent forms of research, but always while acting out alternative scenarios. Costumed and intoxicated by the release/danger that is anticipated, the barker as knowing shaman draws others in by setting the stage for breakthough stories and for further breakout experiences to be shared. The barker is the cocreator and purveyor of dreams, visions, mandalas, symbols, role-playing, and poetry. Performance belongs to all and provides the catalyst for ongoing arts-based inquiry—it enables us to go beyond the usual norms and to make more of our selves and of our history (Cancienne, 1999).

The barker as a leader? Yes, an eclectic and integrative one. Consider how the Hebrew word for *prophet, navi,* first meant to bark (as from the wilderness) and then to proclaim, say more, call, or summon (see *Encyclopaedia Britannica,* 1999). Unlike traditional authority figures, the barker-prophet claims no personal or particular part in the utterance other than to bark/draw attention to, resembling an instrument on which others play. The barker highlights the texts (works and contributions) of others rather than relegating them to the margins of his/her own main text. The barker's role, then, is to attract the audience to the midway as an invigorating cultural site where new forms of educational research can be invented and played out. The public arena as a carnival—a postmodern public arena in which members of all ranks/types can speak/perform freely? In postmodern times, the carnival transcends the village square, the coffeehouse, and the stage (Adair, 2000). The carnival provides a safe space for trying out new and daring forms of inquiry and research relationships.

Conceptually the postmodern carnival acts as an "in-between" place that provides boundary conditions where something new and breathtaking can always be triggered. Creative tensions are generated between such different states as the outmoded and the not yet. During the riotous, "no-holds-barred fling" of carnival, postmodern arts-based inquiry authorizes us to question all modernist myths and to queer all norms. Temporally the postmodern carnival is also an "in between" time coming after or in spite of the bleakness of empiricism and before what we cannot really anticipate. Already we hear that fewer schools have full-time art teachers and that the "standards" mentality and its standardizing testing mania (empiricism) are eliminating the arts in more schools and reducing diversity across teacher and student populations. Especially during these times of superficial political barking about, for example, the redeeming value of national tests, we need as artistic inquirers to gather along the midway, pitching our tents and offering our wares as breakout barkers. Dreaming our data. Dancing our dance our own way, while promoting others' experimental movements.

Watch How the Barker Works the Crowd

The setting/billing was changing, during the time of our performance, from the Curriculum and Pedagogy Conference to the Arts-Based Educational Research (ABER) Conference. Thus our performance literally marked the in-between space of two shows, and ours was subsequently rendered as an all too rushed dress rehearsal, getting underway 20 minutes later than we had expected, leaving us with only 40 minutes for the show. In the restless unease of a paradigmatic "in-between" time and with attendance numbers dwindling during the crossover time of the two conferences, we anticipated playing to an empty room like Barth's (1968) abandoned funhouse.

Strutting in a gaudy jacket and high heels, Carol Mullen advertised the "alluring starlit woman" while projecting carnival images and playing carousel music to draw a crowd. In the meantime Patrick Diamond, with tropical shirt hanging loose and partly open, and flaunting his manly appeal, lured the conference participants into entering our tent (room) by touting as barker in the nearby dining hall. In the role of circus performer/announcer, he invited potential troupe members to finish their lunchtime conversations and to join "the greatest show on earth!"

We set up the room as a series of circus tent acts. And as the carnival metaphor challenges non-admission to forbidden zones and releases us from conventions, so, in this spirit, each carnival visitor had to select a ticket from a fanned stack that Carol held out in order to gain entry into our tent. The roundtables, identified with nametags, beckoned troupe members, inviting them to re-imagine themselves and educational research as they chose their table and role from the dizzying choices among *The Illusionists, The Trapeze Fliers, The Jugglers, The Tight-Rope Walkers, The Tumbling Acrobats, The Untamed Animals,* and *The Fire-Eaters!* And, then, we assume, they privately entertained what this unusual approach to teaming and reflection might mean to them. Eleven people entered the tent and joined our circus show.

Stories of Breakthrough and Breakout

Although his groundbreaking classic texts have defined the field of art-based research, Eisner (e.g., 1997) may be seen, as by Slattery (1995), as a modernist who is "really a transitional figure in the emerging aesthetic curriculum field" (p. 212). We seek to be more transgressive and freely collaborative. We now breakout ourselves by representing the performances of the troupe at and after the carnivalesque session. Again we seek to act as encouraging educational barkers rather than as critics judging the quality of the performances and reflections of the troupe. We present the data as a group performance with selected solos and *pas de deux* dancing multiple breakthrough and breakout stories.

Individuals at the session shared stories, poems, reflections, and free-form sketches—all carnival-like mini-performances that we helped to initiate with our program guide. We were delighted that so many of the troupe were so forthcoming. They were able to play openly outside the closed box of expected roles as conference goers and educational researchers. While some of the troupe participants offered their reflections during the session, others shared theirs later. We reconstruct selections of both here. On the handout outlining the carnival activities, we anticipated that some of the troupe would strongly resonate with and rebel against the image of having been "trained" as traditional empiricists—almost as animals held captive in a zoo or traveling menagerie. We sought to enlist their imagination as carnival performers so as to help us to all find ways to "dance" our data in a series of fast-paced but thoughtful turn-taking moves.

Invitation: Awaking to an A-wake

To create opportunities for new educational research experiences at the session, we framed the session by eliciting responses to four provocative questions:

- What finally killed off empirical educational research or content-only, top-down teacher education programs for you?
- Who or what delivered the "death blow"?
- When did you first recognize that there was an arts-based alternative?
- What examples or forms of inquiry convinced you that this was a viable/inevitable approach?

By launching an intriguing scenario, we set the conditions for the PABER show and the sharing of breakthrough and breakout stories. This opening act suggested a wake or funeral: "Picture yourself as invited to attend a post-mortem wake for the passing of empirical educational research and also a launch-party for Postmodern Arts-Based Educational Research (PABER)." Next, we read a joint poem of ours called "Art Takes Its First Awkward Steps" (in Diamond & Mullen, 1999, pp. 449–450). This transgressive piece celebrates both the death of empiricism and the birth of arts-based inquiry:

Who's dead?
A new dug grave awaits
The in-ter(ra)nment of the pre-post body.
Its main part took a fatal blow.
Life ar-rested post-haste. Rigor mortis.
Stayed too long at its post. The last post.
"Pass the body bag, please."

Over the broken modernist body
the postmodernist "monster" now lurches.
the creation and not the Baron!
Another stitched together Frankenstein,

Postpartum, a body of opinion fears that,
even attaining fullness, the arts
cannot put/keep body and soul together.

The post-body etherized upon a slab of marble.
Time for its predelivery inspection,
the body cavity search, the logosectomy,
the dire-gnosis, and then out into the word-world.

Art takes its first awkward steps as inquiry,
gasping, lurching forth, stretching newfound limbs,
a patchquilt of ill-fitting parts.
Head, heart, fingers, and tail
all cast out from the dying zone.

This poem provided both a warm-up and a foreshadowing of the audience's sharing of individual stories of coming to "a-wake(n)" from the trance induced by transmissive forms of empirical research to the wide-awakeness of arts-based inquiry. Patrick presented this travesty of a poem dramatically (and with accompanying commentary) as a pastiche, a thing of shreds and patches, as Shakespeare's young Hamlet had described his murderous and usurping uncle, Claudius.

As postmodern carnivalesque barker-leaders, we had set our allusive and irreverent treatment of educational research in a graveyard, which then was mysteriously transformed into an operating room. We reflected with the participants on the death (perhaps exaggerated for the sake of spectacle in both meanings of vision and exhibition) of the modernist myth of educational research and teacher development, and on the birthing (much anticipated) of the new stories.

Our parody of a eulogy released/intimated many possibilities. A troupe member who picked up on the farcical or "MASH"-like elements of the poem further stretched the newfound limbs of PABER. For her, the poem confirmed that quantitative approaches to data collection and analysis are well past their "use by" date and truly at the end of their shelf-life—too modernist and still lingering in a postmodern age. Another responded to the poem's evocations of the Frankenstein/Prometheus myth by spontaneously jumping in and reading aloud from our handout/playbill:

> The limbs and tissues of postmodernism overlap at the edges, eschewing "the neat mutually exclusive, jointly exhaustive groupings so clearly desired by modern social science" (Rosenau, 1992, p. 16). Teacher (educator) researchers are now able to cobble together their own risk-defying versions of teaching and teacher selves.

After reading and responding to "Art Takes Its First Awkward Steps," we invited the troupe to read another poem, with spontaneous turn-taking, called "No School on Saturday" by Peter Petrasek. Because the poem does not appear here in full, we paraphrase the author's self-proclaiming project: as artist-teacher he portrays himself in the third person—as the teacher that (he thinks) his students see. This unrehearsed group performance was like the performance of a series of somersaulting aerialists each reaching confidently for the hands of their catchers, their group safety net.

For this reading, the troupe each shared aloud one or more lines from the poem, only as they felt moved to, without any preassignment from the group or ourselves. The troupe seemed intuitively to trust the activity, they, we, at times emphasizing a particular word, or repeating a phrase on their own initiative, or overlapping with a previous reader's line. We also joined in the performance. We noted that some made gestures when reading, such as the troupe member who read "Just a few rocks for a peace garden" with her arms cradling and forming a circle protectively in front of her heart. At no time was there a need to cue anyone to contribute to the reading or, conversely, to restrain anyone from monopolizing it. The troupe performed smoothly and unrehearsed. We experienced the synergy and power of a group performance formed around the subtleties of implicit understandings of stories of teaching and research. These personally resonating stories were intimated as people selected a line to read and articulate in a certain way, such as the *Untamed Animal* who chose to read "'We spend too much time indoors,' . . . 'Too much time sitting at desks'" with penetrating and sardonic emphasis. In PABER, we are released from the pressure of having to act or draw like fully accomplished artists. Instead, we only need to hang-out/in with our authentic experience and to represent it in whatever ways we can, drawing breath, courage, and inspiration from each other.

As the troupe shared experiences and made new connections, they also sketched spontaneously on the notepads we provided during the session (these images are animations in our publication on the CD-ROM). They also made connections to other "works" that they had been interacting with, such as novels and the arts-based literature.

Following from the reading of the two poems and the four questions posed and with very little coaxing, the troupe assumed their new *carny* roles and spoke freely and in some depth of their breakthrough stories. Some even picked up on each other's energy and spun their threads further, sometimes sharing their stories, always eager to hear each others' stories, concerned less with where the conversation was supposed to be going than with savoring the moment and what it might become through improvisation and collaboration.

A *Tumbling Acrobat* shared his initial breakthrough story. In contrast to the discussion that Peter Petrasek's poem had triggered, of how traditional research with its "No Trespassing" sign bans the self and the arts from research, he recalled more open memories of "chemistry at school." With the role of uncertainty readily acknowledged, he had experienced science not as a barrier to but as a catalyst for his love of the arts. Chaos theory had provided him with the freedom to connect to his self, and to his own way of being. He chose to make the arts his life. Because of this experience, he had never really felt that he was blocked in the academy or that his professional growth had been threatened in any way. We also noted that this arts-based leader had chosen an appointment to an arts academy where personal and community-based expression is celebrated in a vigorous outreach program. Operating like a traveling carny busker, this participant does not have to rely on empirical research for survival.

A *Trapeze Flier* rushed up directly after our truncated session to share his breakthrough story. Breathlessly, he said that his "options and tools" for engaging others had been expanded (reframed) as a result of our carnival showcase. He realized that the educational inquirer can begin deliberately with a theoretical research frame and infuse the entire performance with it, rather than beginning and ending organically, hoping participants will gain something of value after having been bombarded with many fragments. He added that others at his workshops had urged him "to land that plane." He reflected further:

> *. . . today you celebrated arts-based inquiry with us, which is the next step I can now see our community needed to make, a step beyond justification and talk about metaphor to the enactment of it. You provided a research framework, one that is invitational and open, and enabled us to internalize it whereas I work the other way around, facilitating the experience and just hoping that my students and participants will just "get" some research meaning and value. I can now see how I can differently engage my own students and audiences, and use the research frame in an organic but explicit way, one that enables others to freely make connections while guiding them at the same time.*

An *Illusionist* responded to our presentation at length, writing self-reflexively in order to spark insights into her development as a researcher. She described her breakthrough/breakout in the guise of a story/fable, "Dressing up on Saturday Night":

> *We are about to begin our favorite ritual, dressing up. I place a dining room chair in front of the mirror. Roslyn, my sister, sits down and I drape a towel around her. I leave the make-up cabinet ajar for easy access to my mother's magical potions. I take cream [which] feels cool, refreshing, and soothing as I dip my fingers into the jar and apply a thin layer to Roslyn's face. Absolute concentration is required. Next, I squeeze a quarter-size circle of beige foundation into the palm of my hand. I place a dot of this creamy substance on Roslyn's forehead, both cheeks, and her chin. Then I join the dots, blending the foundation. I pat on too much face powder, giving her a dreadfully pale look. To give her some color, I brush browny red rouge onto her cheekbones. My hand is unsteady, and the liner is bumpy and high off her eyelids. When I am done, she smiles, and it's my turn.*

This participant's childhood experience of dressing up in order to pass for and feel like an adult parallels the grown-up experience many of us know so well of creating false layers—pretending to be a "hard nosed" and convincing traditional researcher. The "foundation," which is constituted by beige make-up in this account, is applied to the person from the outside, and its effect is pale inauthenticity. The author confirmed our intuitive reading of the piece from her experience of having been conditioned to present a false image to the school/academy. Testing? Step this way? Carnival mirrors? Distortions and reversals of self? Glimpses of the researcher self through childhood stories? Elusive and convoluted, the carnival metaphor reminds us of our deeper self *and* of its endless development:

This participant later responded in writing that the carnival session had helped to "make visible the previously unseen," that dimension of "dressing up" as a researcher that came through her autobiographical sharing and the following reflection for which she draws on quotes from *The Postmodern Educator* (Diamond & Mullen, 1999):

> *Your session certainly did what you set out to do: You "seek to provide permissive and supportive space where we can all write and test our boundaries" (p. 266). You encouraged us to take up the challenge to use our "own language of subversion within dominant forms of knowledge" (p. 275) and to adopt "outlaw perspectives in the shift from the condition of imprisonment to that of self-awareness." This helped me to "make visible the previously unseen," and to "break out of the claustrophobia of confinement" of empirical research. (p. 275)*

A *Tight-Rope Walker* admitted that for her the breakthrough followed her reading of Eisner's (1979) *The Enlightened Eye*. She made the following observations about the sesssion:

> *The tight-rope walker was the metaphor that spoke most directly to my own experience. In the last few years, I've become a pretty good tight-rope walker as I try to balance (and integrate) my two lives. But I do sense that I am trying to live two lives. It's an ongoing struggle that requires divisions of my day. I'm always trying to find moments for consulting the poet, allowing her vision to inform the academic work. It's never enough. . . . I love your elaboration on the carnival theme. The explicit distinction between "gatekeeper" and "barker" seems important and elucidating. And the etymological information that leads to "prophet-barker" is marvelous.*

A second *Untamed Animal,* a graduate student at an institution that supports arts-based inquiry, offers the rich insight that not everyone has experienced a breakthrough moment in response to the old paradigm of empirical research. In asking this question, we had of course mistakenly assumed that everyone had been shackled or tamed: *"There was never any moment when I gave up on or turned away from the old paradigm because I was never in it to begin with."* Not everyone had previously been forced just to dance to someone else's tune.

Finally a *Fire-Eater* wrote that the experience of having been restrained by the academy and of being released through arts-based inquiry was a very real and transformative one for her. This contributor offers the perspective that, if arts-based research began with the need empirically to prove itself by demonstrating that "the arts measurably improve learning outcomes," its more recent developments respect unpredicted outcomes, exploration, invention, and the dance of the "whole self":

> *Your session gives voice to all that I have been believing, doing, and saying for several years. It is so clear and resonates so much, especially the parts about being dismissed and oppressed for using a different form of research. THANK YOU for helping to legitimate our work within the public spaces of the academy. I also felt validated for exploring and inventing arts-based methodology. It is very powerful (and empowering for ME) to realize that I am part of a movement. I now know that when I am trying to be my artistic, whole self I am not alone. The breakthrough occurred for me when I refused to do an empirical doctoral study, which basically was to "prove" that the arts improve learning outcomes!*

The Final Curtain Call in Our PABER Show

Due to the crossover between the Curriculum and Pedagogy and ABER conferences our performance had to be closed off abruptly. The tent came crashing down. Nevertheless as the comments testify, the members of the troupe clearly valued having been cast and transported, however briefly, as "carnival performers and animals" in our circus tent. The reduced one-hour slot allocated for our performance could only have been, as one participant's pun suggested, "a taste of what can be unleashed in the academy"—or what is possible when we authorize spontaneous role-playing and other performative elements as in a carnival-like experience.

Further, instead of assessing the value of the session in terms of the high expectations that we had personally held for it, we have reframed our intentions here using the metaphor of "performance as rehearsal," and its reversal, "rehearsal as performance" (Diamond = Mullen, 2000). When we come to pitch our tent in the next town, we will again perform as barkers at a dress rehearsal, but with a firmer schedule and more synergy. Even "the free-form processive dance" (Slattery, 1995, p. 28) of postmodern arts-based educational research that is so rich in indeterminacy, disequilibrium, and lived experience needs rigor and imagination if it is to take flight joyfully.

At a future event that we are planning for another ABER conference, we fully expect to be able to play more fully with the carnivalesque spirit, although perhaps with a less ambitious "agenda" and within an expanded time-slot. When we have done this, we will be able to report more fully on what is triggered when participants experience all of the roundtable and whole group activities. At that time, we hope to be able to offer insights as performed in our finale. This will be staged by inviting members at each roundtable to share their arts-based practices/creations and to enact their assigned/self-declared roles. Human cannonballs may be "shot" as more magicians and clowns gambol and disport themselves. Bellying to their full heights along the midway, the marquees will be all freshly painted, multi-hued, and festooned with lights. They will be flanked by a riot of booths hawking food, trinkets, and tickets for games, carousels, rides, and mirror mazes.

After our PABER session, we imagined our role of educational barker as a more outrageous parody of the inquirer, the gypsy fortune-teller. In Barth's (1968) version the gypsy is a mechanical figure trapped behind glass. We know this gypsy fortune-teller because we have played her too, trapped in the booth of empirical and traditional research with its cracked and taped glass windows. Like hers, our "kerchiefs and silks [may seem] long-faded" (p. 85). But these trappings/colors are the arts, dance, and the humanities being finally being restored to educational research. New steps to an age-old dance that dares vertigo!

Reflections such as these on our performance raise a series of questions. Does arts-based inquiry, and especially our version of it that we have announced as Postmodern Arts-Based Educational Research (PABER), always end up trapping us as a pair of made-up carnival barkers promising more than we can deliver? Or, is it the misperception of others of arts-based inquiries as weird or narcissistic that produces the trap? A third possibility, and the one that our circus show demonstrated, is that the modernist myth of educational research itself is the trap—thankfully postmodernism suggests the means for seeking release by performing counter/alternative stories/moves and selves. Perhaps we can become like a gypsy oracle rummaging though our ragbag for literary and remembered scraps to illustrate our ideas/premonitions.

To free our artistry daily, we may need to take on the role of "tumbling acrobats," "illusionists," or fortune-telling gypsies, for example, as a way to "play with and invest feeling in external images of self" (Sennett, cited in Adair, 2000, p. 12). Carnival provides a public space for us as art-based researchers to congregate and to bring together what have previously been only our privately transgressive selves.

For the PABER session, we generated the occasion and structures for researchers to explore arts-based experimentation. Our research project strives for greater acceptance of and even legitimacy within the academy for arts-based work that is textual and based on live performance (offered in makeshift tents). We all know that the old cover story/moves of educational research will no longer do and that the new stories/moves are not yet fully or regularly in place, but we can take advantage of this postmodern crossover to search for new forms of arts-based educational research that can take hold, even if only fleetingly. We hope that glimpses of this work have shone through here.

Notes

1. As art-based alternative collaborators we have replaced the traditional "&" symbol with "=" between our names to suggest a new inquiry relationship symbolizing genuine equal authorship. Carol A. Mullen initiated this new practice with another feminist colleague (see Mullen = Kochan, 2001).

References

Adair, D. L. (2000, November). The fall of the public academic. Provocation offered for the inaugural Annual Meeting of the Conference on Curriculum and Pedagogy, Austin, TX.

Barth, J. (1968). *Lost in the funhouse.* New York: Doubleday.

Bateson, M. C. (1990). *Composing a life.* New York: Penguin Books.

Cancienne, M. B. (1999). The gender gaze: Rethinking gender through performance. *Journal of Curriculum Theorizing, 15*(2), 167–175.

Diamond, C. T. P. = Mullen, C. A. (2000). Rescripting the script: Taking research to the "edge of the exploratory." *International Journal of Education & the Arts* [On-line serial], 1(4), 1–23. Available: http://ijea.asu.edu/vln4

Diamond, C. T. P., & Mullen, C. A. (Eds.). (1999). *The postmodern educator: Arts based inquiries and teacher development.* New York: Peter Lang.

Eisner, E. W. (1979). *The enlightened eye* (1st ed.). New York: Macmillan.

Eisner, E. W. (1997). The promise and perils of alternative forms of data representation. *Educational Researcher, 26*(6), 4–10.

Encyclopaedia Britannica CD. (1999). Chicago, IL. [On-line]. Available: http://www.eb.com

Hawking, S. W. (1988). *A brief history of time: From the big bang to black holes.* New York: Bantam Books.

Heaney, S. (1996). *Death of a naturalist.* London: Faber & Faber.

Jipson, J., & Wilson, B. (1997). TH AT DIA LOG UE AT NI GHT. In J. Jipson & N. Paley (Eds.), *Daredevil research* (pp. 161–183). New York: Peter Lang.

Jipson, J., & Paley, N. (2000). Because no one gets there alone: Collaboration as co-mentoring. *Theory into Practice, 39*(1), 36–42.

Marcus, G. E. (1994). What comes (just) after "post"?: The case of ethnography. In N. K. Denzin & Y. S. Lincoln (Eds.), *Handbook of qualitative research* (pp. 563–574). London: Sage Publications.

Mullen, C. A., & Diamond, C. T. P. (2001, Summer). Performances in arts-based inquiry. [Guest editors' special issue]. *Journal of Curriculum Theorizing, 17*(2).

Mullen, C. A. = Kochan, F. K. (2001). Issues of collaborative authorship in higher education. *The Educational Forum, 65* (2), 128–135.

Rosenau, P. M. (1992). *Post-modernism and the social sciences: Insights, inroads, and intrusions*. Princeton, NJ: Princeton University Press.

Slattery, P. (1995). *Curriculum development in the postmodern era.* New York: Garland.

Weber, M. (1946). The social psychology of the world religions. In H. H. Gerth & C. Wright Mills (Eds.), *From Max Weber: Essays in sociology* (pp. 267–301). New York: Oxford University Press. (Original work published 1919)

CHAPTER 10

Artistic Inquiry: On Lighthouse Hill

GENE DIAZ

This is the place where our spirits commune, where we can hear with shared delight the noises of the soul in play.
—hooks, *Wounds of Passion*

In searching for a way of describing what we do, I have arrived at this place between art and inquiry to dig for details, notice nuances, and engage in the creative process of writing. I create inquiry as I do art, and know art as inquiry. This is not to say that the two are exclusive of one another, not at all; they can be seen as the same process from different perspectives, utilizing disparate discourses. The challenge is to bring together art and inquiry by coordinating the two discourses. Within this chapter I continue to bridge the gap between art and science, a gap forced into existence, like some rift in the earth following a jarring earthquake, following the Age of Enlightenment, the deification of Descartes, and the dawning of the supremacy of positivistic science.

The process of scientific inquiry involves seeking to know the world in new ways, from different perspectives, with added depth of detail and fresh insight. As researchers we engage in this systematic process based upon formats, methods, and ideologies shaped into distinct methodologies, thus meeting the criteria for a general consensus of researchers. As artists we engage in a similar systematic process based upon formats and methods which we ourselves create, and which define the criteria of each of us as creators within a community of artists. The processes of artistic creation and scientific inquiry are in many ways similar, yet at the same time they rest in distinct discursive worlds maintained as separate and inequitable. Perhaps Kristeva's (1980) dual signifying processes that are involved in any production of meaning, semiotic and symbolic, point us to the intersection and interconnection of these two fields of study. Science and art cross, intersect, imitate, and assimilate one another in both sign and symbol. In ways that are distinct they cause us to change (Naum Gabo, 1937: "Science teaches, Art asserts. Science persuades, Art acts" [in Herbert, 1964, p. 103]).

Here I juxtapose these disparate discourses, specifically those of ethnography and painting, through a discursive collage of meaning-making in my words as ethnographer and those of John Dehlinger, painter. In doing this I assume that meaning is constituted discursively in the intersection of self/subjectivity and the social relations of society. Meaning is temporally located, and always being contested, negotiated and transformed, while appearing to remain the same. The different discursive fields of art and research employ different ways of making meaning of the world, of constructing reality. Both John and I are negotiators of meaning and translators of experience; we both attempt to know the world anew through processes of inquiry; we both construct layers of meaning and utilize everyday objects in our processes of creating reality and illusion; we both reflect and critique in a recursive dialogue with ourselves and the world. Just as the nature of the social world is the focus for our work as social science researchers, the nature of art serves as the main concern of artists (Alberro, 2000).

This discursive collage combines text from the artistic process with text from an ethnographic inquiry, in the same way that visual collage mixes painted images with real objects. Collage combines our everyday reality—bits of photographs, newspaper, found objects from everyday life—with paint or ink, thus merging the illusionary with the actual, art with society, aesthetics with everyday/everynight life. Both in the visual and the discursive, this double stage effect, or overlay of text/images, promotes "a drama of two realities enacting on two levels of experience" (Janis & Blesh, 1967, p. 13). As with the drama of the two realities of artists/researchers coming together to share their arts-based inquiries while at the same time engaging in the process of artistic inquiry, this collage combines the drama of the process of painting with the search for knowledge through ethnographic inquiry.

The discursive collage that follows allows images of Lighthouse Hill on Monhegan Island to surface and become visible as they float over and under textual references. The words of painter John

Dehlinger, as he talks about the process and methods of creating the egg-tempera painting *Lighthouse Hill,* are intersected with text from an ethnography of a creative arts high school. Images from Lighthouse Hill, on the small island off the coast of Maine where Jamie Wyeth lived and painted for many years, intersect and overlay images of a public high school for the arts in New Orleans. Words of researchers and artists about these processes overlap and struggle for a compositional place within these two descriptive discourses. One question that recurs in my work and that of other artists and researchers is the one we ask ourselves when we feel a need to clarify ourselves for our colleagues. What is it that I am doing, and why do I do this? John begins by addressing this question.

This desire to make marks . . . is what I do. Make marks on a surface. All kinds of people like to make marks, kids make marks with spray cans on subways. I only wanted to make my marks all the time—making marks said something about me.

I can only write about the knowledge I, myself, gain through my participation in an investigation, and my knowing is limited by my interpretive style and background, i.e., by who I am. I am directly related to and embedded in my work. My need to understand the work of artists in schools derives from my own efforts as an artist in education.[1]

That's the process that describes the world as I see it. The marks, on some level, become something else. It's when you get the paint to be paint and something else at the same time, clouds, trees, flesh . . . or it relates to something else . . . when you're describing a grassy hillside and you look at it and you say, "Hey that looks like velvet." So that you're not only getting that it is grassy hillside, and you're saying that with those marks, but you're now leading the viewer, and yourself as the primary viewer . . . to seeing something else in there. Seeing something else. Relating to something. All of this is like velvet, this is like a soft folded napkin, and it's not that, it's a hillside. . . . Through your painting it then refers to something else. It's a referral thing.

I find, like Spradley (1980), that ethnography is not studying people, but rather learning from people. To gain access to this perspective, I must gain the confidence of a group, learn the language and the customs of the members, and lessen the cultural distance between me and the group members. It's important, as Woods (1986) says, that the language of the members be visible in the language of the researcher. Thus, I began to speak the discourse of the artist/teachers, and found myself recognized more and more as a participant in their work.

I think of the really great painters, like Rembrandt—if you look at Rembrandt's painting it may be a portrait of a woman, but there are parts of it that refer to lots of other things that would bring to mind, or bring forth from you an association of—something that he's not describing in the painting.

Since ethnography is the study of a culture, a learning process for me is at the core of this coming to terms. This is a deeply interpretive process and represents my attempt to understand a culture in a similar fashion to those that live within it. This learning process meant acknowledging what I didn't know about the experience of being an artist in a public school.

You get to know it in a completely different way than what you thought you knew it as. Your entire perspective on something changes. It's that kind of joy that keeps me painting. There's a joy in painting. There's a joy that say I'm doing something that I've never done before. I'm discovering. This is now informing me about something else. Something that I was completely unaware of. The best work that I've done almost has a surreal quality somewhere in the paint, and to me . . . to me I'm the most important viewer of that painting . . . and that painting has to work for me on a whole bunch of different levels, or I'll get rid of it.

As an ethnographer I understand that my presence in any situation influences others around me. Recognizing this prompts reflection on the ways my actions as a researcher influence others in the research site. Louise, the dance teacher, needed to make me aware of the damaging comments of previous observers in her class that reflected their ignorance of the intensity of work the students engaged in.

So there's a need that's in there somewhere, and that's the part that I don't really understand. There's a feeling of need that I have to do this, that I have to go make these marks. The process is really important. That's why I paint in egg tempera, because the process is so important for that technique. The actual process of how you do the eggs, how you stick the paint on, how you make the panel, all that is very, very important.

Ethnography is characteristically reflexive; that is, I acknowledge my position as part of the social world being studied (Hammersley & Atkinson, 1983). Ethnographic text does not simply report an independent order of reality; it is not neutral. Rather, it is the construction of a reality through the use of rhetorical and textual devices. The text I write involves the construction of the reality of a culture, a school, a classroom, through the reflexive application of critical insights (Atkinson, 1990). This recursive process of coming to know and represent a reality must somehow be transparent for the reader of my work. I must ask if the artist/teachers are seen through my words.

Now, in the process, I'll do a whole number of drawings, at some point in time. . . . Lighthouse Hill was made up of the first drawing . . . in more of a landscape format, more of a horizontal format, with Peg walking up the hill. The lighthouse was in there, that tree was in there, the bell was in there—and that's usually the way my paintings start. They start with a concept that contains lots and lots and lots and lots of things. And then I begin to look at them and say, well, I don't want this thing in there, and I don't want that thing, and I start pulling things out. And often as I'm drawing the format will change.

I am always guessing at meanings, assessing my guesses, and drawing explanatory conclusions from them. Like Geertz (1973), I don't propose to discover the "Continent of Meaning" and map out its bodiless landscape. Each day I visited the school my understanding of the work of artist/teachers changed. I began to see how their work in the normative setting of schooling was in coordination with their work as artists. This changed me.

And so it goes through lots and lots of changes, till finally I think that I'm fairly close to, if I use these elements now that I have left, out of all the ones I've eliminated, and I end up with three elements or four elements I think that those will be the ones that will make the statement. So then I go to the panel, I know the shape of the panel and I know basically what the subject is that's going on that shape. I start working on the actual panel—then begin to draw all the elements on there. Now I get it up to that size, which is maybe four, five, six times bigger than it was in the drawing, it changes dramatically. Now I'll look at that, and often for one or two days I'll look at just the black marks on the white panel to see, "How's that feel? Does that feel like that's right?" It looks okay on a sketch, in the sketchbook, but now you're dealing with something that's four, five, six times bigger.

As an educational researcher I am interested in constructing concepts which help me and other educators better understand the work that artists/teachers do. During the initial phase of this investigation, I developed a holistic understanding of this school, as I devoted much of my efforts toward establishing routes of access to information and gaining the confidence of the faculty. My initial observations in the classrooms where students danced, wrote, acted or painted, sang or played music, were of the atmosphere, the relationships, the environments.

I want to say that this is a particular place, too. It's the Lighthouse Hill on Monhegan. So there has to be something left with that. Maybe it'll be only the rock that she's stepping on, but it isn't, it has to become, it's the tree that's up there, and it's a very distinctive tree. . . . I wanted to maintain the sense of place, but the lighthouse was just in way, way too much competition with her, with the big blocky thing that was part in shadow, and she came out nice and sunny against it. But it didn't make the statement.

The act of writing assumes an attitude of persuasiveness. Literary persuasion, or rhetoric, like much of visual persuasion, is artistic. As writers and painters we try to persuade our readers and viewers to see the world through our eyes. So Barone (2000) cautions us, as the reader/viewer, to maintain vigilance against abuse of authorial power. Initially I assumed that the artists brought unrecognized benefits to the classroom/studio. Later I also discovered that teaching, and their students, enhanced their work as artists.

So then I'm saying, "Well, what the hell is the statement about?" Well, it is about the place. How do I get the place? Well, the place is the bell that was up there, the lighthouse that was up there, the size and shape of the hill, and this old weird looking tree that's up there. And I settled on the tree. I just settled on the tree because as I eliminated things the tree ended up as being one of the things left. So now I have the figure of Peg and I have the tree. To me that pretty much says, that's Lighthouse Hill. The lighthouse for some reason isn't as nearly as symbolic of that hill as that weird tree is—been up there in the wind and been blowing all over the place.

During the second round of visits to the classrooms, I was more familiar with the settings and the participants, and was thus able to focus more attention on particular pedagogical events which took place. It was as if I uncovered another layer of this "problematic." An analogy would be that of walking into a very dark room from out of the sunlight. Once your eyes adjust to the dimness you are able to distinguish the objects in the room. In a similar fashion, once my eyes adjusted to the unaccustomed activities in this public school, I was able to focus more clearly on the pedagogical concepts. Thus the concepts emerged, so to speak, from out of the darkness of my ignorance. I began to notice the ways that the metaphor of the school as family excluded as well as included certain individuals, those that didn't make the cut in the auditions, classroom teachers in the "sending schools."

So I then began to actually work on the hillside, to find out where the shadow patterns are . . . notice some serendipitous thing, one shadow pattern is very much in the shape of her body—I actually enhanced that as I went along, that came in the doing. Lots of things come in the doing. So then I thought, where are all these things that Peg likes? Where are the things that she likes? She loves to pick flowers and stuff like that, and there were no flowers up there. So I decided to put in some rugosa roses in there. . . . I had rugosa roses coming out my ears . . . because again, I like to make marks and sometimes I just get involved in making marks and put marks on top of marks on top of marks. . . . All of a sudden I had too many roses.

Through the interweaving of interpretation and analysis I create a sometimes fragmented and dispersed narrative which disrupts a strict chronology of events. By including my personal narrative with "objective" description I contribute to this fragmentation. By re-ordering the narrative into thematic categories I present the events of social actions as extended examples supporting the analysis of the data. Atkinson (1990) explains this re-ordering thus: "The significance of events is thus found not primarily in their narrative sequence, but in their relations of similarity and difference with other narrative units. In other words, the 'conventional' ethnography places events in paradigmatic relations, rather than the mere recapitulation of their syntagmatic, diachronic relations" (p. 126). Repeatedly the artists emphasized the dilemmas generated by teaching innovation and imaginative expression within a controlling and controlled environment. The discourses of arts and schooling had to be coordinated.

Then I began to take my pile of green paint and go back over the roses. They're still there. Somehow I feel that they inform the surface. The more stuff you do to the panel, even though it's not there and you can't even see it anymore, the more it's gonna inform what's going on. It's all these trial and error things that you do in a painting that somehow inform the totality of the picture that comes out. Even though they don't exist. They existed at another time. You could never see them. They are relevant to the process. I don't think that what you have now would have the same quality if you hadn't gone through the process.

The transition between exploration and reconstruction was a gradual one for me. At times I found myself uncovering new conceptual devices as I discovered new physical places in the school. Discovering the overlapping of the discourses of arts and schooling prompted me to reconsider the process of teaching/learning in this setting as an elaborately choreographed dance. The artist/teachers opened spaces for students as they created them for themselves, feeling blessed with the opportunity for teaching and learning.

So now we're really boiling this thing down—the elements that are left are basically what you see now. The lighthouse is gone, the big bell is gone, the fallen tree is gone, about 80% of the roses are gone. All these things are gone out of it, but somehow they're there, for me they're still there. I still feel them as part of the atmosphere of the place. I'm trying get the feeling of the place and the feeling of this person. The way I feel about this place.

My interpretive style as the writer decides the way that meaning is represented here, and this representation is additionally a self-presentation. That is, the presence of the Other in the text relates to my presence as writer. Sitting in the music classroom listening to the ethereal voice of a 15-year-old girl I notice myself as an enchanted listener by myself as researcher. Who is Other? Who is Self?

About halfway through the painting, and this happens with every painting, I have to look at this and say "Does this work?" I'm gonna be working on this for two or three weeks, maybe four, and is it worth four weeks. . . . Is what I'm after, am I gonna get close enough that it makes it worth four weeks?

Research findings tell stories; stories that can be insightful and useful in shaping what we think and do as educators. Shaping these stories is also a process that shapes us as researchers. We become conceptual palindromes. Making the Other strange means becoming unfamiliar with myself. I wanted to "go native," drop the researcher, move back into the classroom.

I had this really nice shadow and light pattern that looks like the figure. Maybe that's sufficient. . . . So I thought, well, enhance that, so I did . . . still there was no satisfaction. It had to be the figure. So now I get into the problem of . . . what is it I want to say about her? So I had Peg pose for me. And then I thought, what was the thing that most fascinated me the first time I ever saw her? What continues to fascinate me about her? One thing is what I call about Peg, there's an awkward beauty about her. She almost has this ungainly quality of a teenager. She's not graceful, yet she's really graceful. And I thought, I'm after something like that.

Social science meets my personal needs. Both Krieger (1991) and Denzin (1994) make that point in different ways. Kreiger points to abstract thinking as the way different individuals relate to the world. Denzin claims that we are our own subjects. I write of the artist as practicing professional in the classroom, the possibility of learning through doing, knowledge through experience. Bringing their own creation into the classroom, and students into their professional performances, they reinforce the relevance of the educational experience. In this school the student/artists learn by doing.

Then as I did one drawing of her—and I got this ungainly beauty that she has, I had two ways of doing it, coming toward me or going away. . . . I want to say something about this and I don't want to specify her. I want to specify her to me but not to any other viewer. And I want to say something that may be even more general about what I think of as beautiful in a female. Then, just all of a sudden naturally the pink blouse occurred instead of a white one, and the tan pants.

Rational language marginalizes the semiotic aspects of communication. Rational language marginalizes art. Language exceeds the boundaries of both rationality and the symbolic order. The semiotic chora, as Kristeva calls it, is manifest most strongly in such aspects of language as rhythm and intonations and is strongest in non-rational discourses such as poetry and art. Dewey (1958) considers art to be ". . . the greatest intellectual achievement in the history of humanity" (p. 25). Art functions in the service of feeling, breaking down the Cartesian idea of the dualistic nature of humans, and re-establishes the connection between the body and the mind, the senses and the intellectual. Art communicates through qualities, the qualities of our senses.

There's an asymmetrical balance that I'm looking for in a painting, between the main subject matter and whatever else is in the painting. . . . I wanted to make the figure almost as if you cut it out and stuck it on—because it seemed like that would be the statement that this figure is part of the landscape, she's walking over it, and yet, she exists outside of it. That we all do, that we are all part of nature and exist outside of nature. So there were things that went into this that were way beyond what I thought originally.

Meaning is a gerund, like Kokopelli, a changeling. As I attempt to understand through writing, events change my understanding. Garrison (1994) suggests that a unity of events and relatively stable structures is what makes inquiry and research necessary and possible. He proposes the main task of intelligent human effort, and subsequently of educational research, to be "The striving to make stability of meaning prevail over the instability of events" (p. 8). Yet, education as a process defies stability, and the artistic process promotes instability through innovation, imagination, and risk-taking.

Yeah, right, and the way this came about was by . . . communicating with the painting, communicating with what you're doing. Saying, "This is what I want from you, god dammit!" and the painting saying, "This is what I want from you!" And you kind of communicate back and forth, almost like you're working on this living thing. This thing, because it keeps changing, is alive, and it's telling you that this color isn't right, or this color is wrong—or you're not here yet. . . . So then there were a number of things that I did in there. . . . I had that rock all noodled up with little points of light and all kinds of things all over it, and it was beautiful. Like I said, I like to make marks, well they were beautiful marks all over this damn thing. Then I look back at it and I say, well that's not what that painting's about. It's not about that rock. The rock's gorgeous . . . the biggest problem I have then is . . . you have something like that that you like so much, you have the integrity, whatever it is, to take it out, or to push it back.

When practices become text, they are not guarantees of essential truths, or automatic recipes for action, but partial representations of particular discourses. Teitelbaum and Britzman write that we, as researchers (and I add artists) implicate ourselves in larger interests by creating texts and images (1991). Both text and image, and text as image, like Magritte's painting, Ceci n'est pas une pipe, in which the words "this is not a pipe" overlay a painting of a pipe, allow us to make statements about the practice of statement-making.

Basically I spent two days looking much more than I was doing on this painting. With tempera it seems like that's very important. I can paint tempera very fast . . . in the long run I don't paint the picture that fast because I have to stop and look. . . . Say in a sitting of four to six hours I might take just two solid hours of sitting or standing and looking. There's lots of looking that I do . . . upside down, sideways, always look at it in the mirror, and then I have a reducing glass . . . which gives you the main compositional elements. . . . I do that all through the painting, at any step from the beginning on, I'm turning the painting constantly, putting it on its side, putting it upside down, looking at in different lights. I really like looking at it in different lights, that for some reason seems to help me a lot. If the feeling that I get looking at the painting is the same when it's brightly lit as when it's out, then I think I'm onto something. Or if the feeling's similar, so that you can see the main compositional light and dark elements when it gets dimmer and dimmer, if those are saying something similar to something that it does when it's lit . . . then I think the painting is coming along pretty well.

In addition to representing the reality of the school . . . ethnography also represents my own reality, that is, my developing awareness of the events and actions which transpired within the school during my attendance, and the recognition of my own reasons for attendance. I came in order to understand the experiences of the artists in this school, and to be an artist in a school.

You put too damn much time into a tempera . . . having the integrity to take stuff out, or to scrape off the painting, is a very, very important part of the painting. It takes so damn long to do it, that it's very hard to do that . . . but if you're true to yourself, you have to take it out. That's a key element, that when you look at people who do egg tempera painting, that they miss . . . they get something that gets them real excited and they keep on working, and then their painting becomes confused, and off balance, and all kinds of things. But it's a very, very difficult thing to do because you put that amount of time into it. That's the only problem with working with egg tempera, that I find, is that you have such an investment into the painting, amounts of time, that that can be a hindrance to express what you want to express. Detail of the subject matter—all the marks that you've made on there that are important, but that are not even seen. You don't get the experience of doing. The experience of doing, that's part of this painting, it isn't what you finally see, it's the whole process. The reason that I paint is that process. The process is probably why I paint.

My interpretive style stresses emergent designs and emergent understanding, but also includes a critical component. I ask what social effects I want my understanding to have. I find that ethnographic research is a transformative process for both the researcher and the participants. In conversations with the artist/teachers we developed an awareness of the ways that they teach across the curriculum, involve inter/multicultural methods, and create opportunities for students to participate in curriculum as process. We discovered more, and sometimes less, in their teaching and learning experiences that we had anticipated.

A journey without a destination—if you know the destination it's not gonna be very much fun getting there. Along the way you may learn things, but it's not nearly as enjoyable if you don't know. . . . That's what I do in a painting, to start out and not know what my destination is. . . . It keeps the whole thing alive.

The research process . . . changed my conception of what constitutes understanding. Through the process of attempting to understand this school, I conclude that the attempt is itself the process of understanding; that to learn is to continually recognize that you don't know. Once knowledge and understanding can be considered achievements or accomplishments, they will certainly have escaped.

Notes

1. All passages in italics unless otherwise noted are my own words (Gene Diaz).

References

Alberro, A. (2000). Reconsidering conceptual art. *Conceptual art: A critical anthology.* Boston: M.I.T. Press.

Atkinson, P. (1990). *The ethnographic imagination.* London: Routledge.

Barone, T. (2000). *Aesthetics, politics, and educational inquiry: Essays and examples.* New York: Peter Lang.

Cherryholmes, C. (1988). *Power and criticism: Poststructural investigations in education.* New York: Teachers College Press.

Denzin, N. (1994). The art of interpretation, evaluation, and presentation. In N. Denzin & Y. Lincoln (Eds.), *Handbook of qualitative research* (pp. 500–515). Thousand Oaks, CA: Sage.

Denzin, N. K. (1994). Evaluating qualitative research in the poststructural moment: The lessons James Joyce teaches us. *International Journal of Qualitative Studies in Education, 7*(4), 295–308.

Dewey, J. (1958). *Art as experience.* New York: Capricorn Books. (Original work published 1934)

Diaz, G. R. (1994). *Coordinating discourses: An ethnography of a creative arts high school.* Unpublished doctoral dissertation, University of New Orleans, LA.
Foucault, M. (1972). *The archeology of knowledge & the discourse on language.* New York: Pantheon.
Garrison, J. (1994). Realism, Deweyan pragmatism, and educational research. *Educational Researcher, 23*(1), 5–14.
Geertz, C. (1973). Thick description: Toward an interpretive theory of culture. In C. Geertz (Ed.), *The interpretation of cultures: Selected essays* (pp. 3–30). New York: Basic Books.
Hammersley, M., & Atkinson, P. (1983). *Ethnography: Principles in practice.* London: Routledge.
Herbert, R. L. (Ed.). (1964). *Modern artists on art.* Englewood Cliffs, NJ: Prentice-Hall.
hooks, b. (1997). *Wounds of passion: A writing life.* New York: Henry Holt & Co.
Janis, H., & Blesh, R. (1967). *Collage: Personalities, concepts and techniques.* Philadelphia: Chilton Book Co.
Krieger, S. (1991). *Social science and the self: Personal essays on an art form.* New Brunswick, NJ: Rutgers University Press.
Kristeva, J. (1980). *Desire in language: A semiotic approach to literature and art.* New York: Columbia University Press.
Smith, D. (1987). *The everyday world as problematic.* Boston: Northeastern University Press.
Spradley, J. P. (1980). *Participant observation.* New York: Holt, Rinehart, & Winston.
Teitelbaum, K., & Britzman, D. P. (1991). Reading and doing ethnography: Teacher education and reflective practice. In B. R. Tabachnick & K. Zeichner (Eds.), *Issues and practices in inquiry oriented teacher education.* New York: Falmer.
Vygotsky, L. S. (1962). *Thought and language.* Cambridge, MA: M.I.T. Press. (Original work published 1962)
Weedon, C. (1987). *Feminist practice and poststructuralist theory.* Oxford: Basil Blackwell.
Woods, P. (1986). *Inside schools: Ethnography in educational research.* New York: Routledge & Kegan Paul.

CHAPTER 11

Women Myths

Teacher Self-Images and Socialization to Feminine Stereotypes

SUSAN FINLEY

She walks into class wearing a blue suit, the skirt demurely above the knee. Her white silk tee-shirt contrasts nicely with the deep blue and is accented by a thin gold chain, with a cross. She sports about a three-inch heel on a pair of pumps, also accented with a thin gold chain, To someone "in the know" about style and fashion, the label on the chain probably indicates who made the shoes and how much they cost. Her make-up is perfect. Her hair is shoulder-length, bottle-blonde, but the kind that comes from the beauty shop, not the bathroom shower. The only thing that gives away the fact that she is a third-grade teacher is an oversized canvas bag so heavy she can barely handle the weight of the homework projects, grade book, paperback books for tomorrow's literature circles, and other items she's managed to cram inside.

She takes a seat next to a pregnant woman, and they say "hello" to each other and their neighbors in the circle as they prepare for a teacher education class focused on curriculum inquiry. On the young blonde's other side is another young teacher, also in her late twenties. She wears a "Winnie the Pooh" sweatshirt and a pair of khaki slacks. Her ankle socks are carefully cuffed to show the Pooh characters that match the theme of her shirt. A hot pink notebook is open on the table in front of her, ready for work. The only thing that distinguishes her from the suburban mothers of the third-grade students she teaches is an oversized canvas bag so heavy she can barely handle the weight of the homework projects, grade book, paperback books for tomorrow's literature circles, and other items she's managed to cram inside.

In the United States, the popular media figure prominently in shaping a person's identity. Through television, music, movies, newspapers, and magazines, children, youths, women, and men are educated and socialized to certain specific identities that include gender and nationality. These identities are grounded within a set of metanarratives about class, race, gender, age, and sexual orientation and are "implemented in everyday life through a political economy of signs and differences which turn women into commodities, desire into sexuality, and erotic love into pornography" (Denzin, 1991, p. 17).

In public spheres the metanarratives found in cultural myths are further perpetuated and institutionalized through legal, economic, and educational forums. Without doubt, schools reinforce the elements of identity formation sustained by popular media. Teachers, like everyone else, have shaped their identities to some greater or lesser extent in the waves of images formed in their daily encounters with the media. Cultural myths, values, and meanings are lived into existence and marketed in consumer goods that are purchased by students, teachers, and parents and brought into schoolhouses. The influence of advertising campaigns that turn youthfulness and femininity into commodities is evident in even a quick survey of the clothing styles, food, and music that are popular in any school building. Schools continue the informal socialization to gender that the media introduce through their participants' casual interactions in popular culture events and the "hidden curriculum" of schools, but cultural metanarratives are also continued by the more formal structures of curriculum and schoolhouse rituals.

My purpose in the inquiry reported here has been to identify some of the popular culture myths about women's identity that are perpetuated in the media, and to discover whether and how these myths are lived out in the identities of female teachers. It has also been my aim to make some assessment of which of these myths are healthy, which are benign, and which spread and continue the cancers of sexist traditions and stereotyping. Teachers' self-images may be a key feature of cultural gender stereotyping and the continuing socialization of students to destructive myths about the roles of women in society. After all, teachers model behaviors for students every day, continually either reinforcing or challenging beliefs and knowledge acquired both in and out of school, through students' participation in families, churches, and neighborhoods, and the all-encompassing media barrage common to twentieth-and twenty-first-century living. Radical revisions of identity perceptions about women in our society require that we take apart the myths—especially those myths that have become intertwined with institutionalized role identities and blind us to understanding the qualities of our own actions and attitudes that endorse their continuation. To end the cycle, we must be able to see ourselves reflected in the image of the stereotype.

In my investigation of the reproduction in (print) media in the United States of attitudes about women—as they are played out by teachers—I began by raising questions specifically focused on stereotypes of female gender identity. How do the media portray women? Do female teachers reproduce and model stereotypes of female identity? What are some of the institutional processes that create and sustain gender categories? Addressing these questions required both textual analysis of media images of women and life history analysis of teachers' experiences of female identity in schools. First, I analyzed (print) media depictions of women. Next, I categorized common media representations of women as metaphors for women's identity, and I cast those metaphors in the visual form of collages. Then, I presented the metaphors to practicing teachers to elicit life story accounts of teachers' experiences of these metaphors in the contexts of schools and teaching. Finally, working from the teachers' life stories, in the context of foundations courses in teacher education, we—the teacher/participants and I—entered a critical dialogue about occurrences of gender roles, cultural stereotyping, and myth reproduction in curriculum and teaching practices. Through this chapter and the accompanying CD I intend to continue and extend that dialogue.

Because the focus of this book, *Dancing the Data,* is on the methods of arts-based research, with respect to that primary task and with regard to the limitations of space, I will refrain from storytelling in this chapter. In particular, the narrative accounts of teachers' experiences of teachers' feminine identity and gender stereotyping will be saved for another day, as will my commentary on my conversations with teachers in which we engaged in critical discourse about myth reproduction and gender stereotyping in schools. Here, in the traditional, written text of this book, I include only a brief descriptive overview of the types of responses returned in my inquiry. The accompanying CD track is a multimedia collage that includes the visual metaphors I used to provoke reflection and inquiry among teacher participants, print and vocal (re)statements from teachers' stories, and a musical interpretation of the overlap between women's images as they are played out in popular culture and reproduced in the schools. Computer technology makes it easier to accomplish the production of an art that does not intend to represent, but rather emerges from a conscious desire to engage in a dialogical narrative which is simultaneously pictorial, verbal, poetic, and musical.

Portraiture as Visual Metaphor

As an educator and collagist, I have constructed life history paintings/collages of teachers, teacher educators, and homeless youth participants in my educational inquiry projects. Constructing collages requires a peculiar level of intimacy with images in popular culture and a critical approach to understanding the assumptions and attitudes that are symbolized in the print media (Finley, 2001).

My primary resource for material for my collaged life history images has been popular magazines—publications any consumer can find on a newsstand. During the past three years, as I have leafed through these publications for the purpose of culling images from their pages to cut and paste into my collages/paintings, I have made notes and kept clippings to try and identify and understand the images (and myths and common portrayals) that popular culture perpetuates about the roles and identities of women. Working from my notes about print media, movie, and television images of women, but primarily relying on hundreds of magazine art clippings, I created twelve visual images of particularly often-recurring popular culture metaphors for female identity. My next step was to present the idea of reproduction of cultural norms to practicing teachers. I asked them to assess the twelve metaphors I had identified and to report whether they could see themselves, their colleagues, or teachers they had known when they were themselves students in school. I invited them to "tell a story that includes a detailed description of the teaching practices you associate with the image you have chosen." I asked: "What do we see? Hear? Taste? Feel?"

My purpose in this exercise was to try and determine whether or not teachers perceive these or other cultural images and gender stereotypes at play in educational settings, and I was interested in learning whether teachers would join me in assuming that schools actively reproduce cultural myths and stereotypes and perpetuate patriarchal dominance. All of the teachers whose stories I sought to obtain were students in master's level teacher education classes that I was teaching. Because modes and methods of self-reflection constitute one of several integrated threads across the curriculum in courses I teach, I was also interested in learning whether teachers whose attention is focused on practicing skills of self-reflection as a research method would analyze their stories in ways that would facilitate self-study of their own teaching practices. By stressing the notion that personal identity is a social construction, achieved despite and because of, or in reproduction of, cultural myths, scripts, and practices, I entertained this project out of hopefulness that as teacher/participants recognized their own reiterations of negative inherited scripts about women's lives, they would be encouraged to rewrite themselves, and to create new social texts that re-construct schooling images that might function to undermine a patriarchal system of domination and control.

In this work, the female body is both the domain for inquiry and the location for emancipation (see also Finley, 2001). "The body—what we eat, how we dress, the daily rituals through which we attend to the body—is a medium of culture," says Susan Bordo (1993/1997, p. 90). Similarly, in his excellent book, *Schooling as a Ritual Performance,* Peter McLaren (1999) introduces the concept of "enfleshment," where social metaphors become inscribed in the persons of students. "Discourse of the body reflects particular ways of seeing (e.g., classifying, ordering, and valuing) that have been produced through institutional, economic, and ethical practices situated within particular technologies of power," writes McLaren (1999, p. 277). Because our ways of seeing are produced in the context of social discourse, the cultural inscriptions of that discourse in/on our bodies correspond with ideas of what it means to be female (Wittig, 1992/1997). Thus, inquiry into the symbolic body-text opens access to the meta-texts of society. Meanwhile, by questioning the import of these meta-texts inscribed in the female form, in this inquiry, I look to the female body as the site of emancipation by analyzing some of the cultural discourse inscribed in the female bodies of teachers. Next, I rewrite those cultural metaphors through the concrete language of the body rendered in the symbolic forms of collage. The collages (both literally and figuratively) tear apart the metaphors that socially orient, normalize, and homogenize the bodies of women, and then reconstruct those metaphors in ways that make it difficult to ignore the constructions of female bodies or to ignore the meanings that we habitually attach to those constructions.

Twelve Women Myths

The artworks created in the first phase of this project consisted of twelve individual panels with painted/collaged images of women that play upon common portrayals of women in popular culture. They are as follows:

1. Gaea

   An earth mother image, responsible for the perpetuation of humankind. She is a powerful figure because it is she who cares for and nurtures others.

2. Dominatrix

   Uses her sexuality to seduce and disarm, but maintains an air of decadence and fun.

3. Good Girl

   Purity personified, she tries to blend in, please others, and avoid the tarnish of conflict. A morally "good" woman, she is "clean" and asexual. She is generally content to forgo any control or power over her own life in order to keep others happy.

4. Princess

   Her delicacy and beauty astound those who see her—she requires a strong man to protect and to save her. She may take unnecessary risks, but men enjoy the rescue.

5. Daughter

   She looks to a father figure as mentor and seeks his approval. Her actions demonstrate her intention to please the boss, or father.

6. Amazon Queen

   A female leader. She may be associated with athleticism and power. We're a little embarrassed about her "masculinity," but we forgive her for it.

7. Lady Liberty

   When deaf, dumb, and blind she can make a pretty good decision—says the myth.
   She welcomes the masses—in her motherly embrace she is the ultimate hostess.
   She is outspoken and forthright. The depiction allows comparisons of the justice icon, the Statue of Liberty, and the Columbia Pictures movie image.

8. Joan of Arc

   She is a woman on a mission. She searches for support among the commoners—the rank and file workers who share her cause.

9. Barbie

   "Pretty Woman" image of a good-times girl who is morally redeemable (just buy her enough clothes).

10. Vamp

   "Dirty" sex for hire. The image is of morally degenerate women who lead men astray from families and productive, "normal" self-identity. If the woman is degraded by her role, that's all right, she asked for it. Includes the Monica Lewinsky types who will "do anything" to be associated with powerful men.

11. Queen

   She is a powerful leader whose strength rests in a strong tradition of respect. In modern examples she wears suits and maintains her power base in corporate or government structures—Margaret Thatcher, Madeleine Albright.

12. Warden

   She is organization personified. Disciplined, strict, stern, and orderly. She is asexual. She attends to the work of teaching, but without softness or stereotypical femininity, and without motherly displays of affection.

Metaphors fix meanings so that they can be deconstructed and their impact understood. To dismantle them is a form of resistance. It was my intention that this process of analyzing socially constructed metaphors could contribute to the project of critical pedagogy, at least by drawing attention to the ways that schooling practices play counterpart to those definitions. The idea is that through increased awareness of perpetuating myths and metaphors, the educational community can interrupt the course of history by actively undermining negative gender images in the larger project of supporting social justice through educational practices.

Critical Stories

In the second phase of this inquiry, teachers explored the patterns and fragments of print matter arranged in my collages, each of which, in turn, provided a central theme around which their stories could be told (Barone, 1992).[1] Because the storytellers each chose one metaphor as the focus of their stories, each of their characterizations became the symbol for an entire set of institutional identities and practices. Thus, in telling their stories, teachers who participated in the inquiry consciously explored the popular culture stereotypes and myths about women's identities that are reproduced in the discourses, practices, and institutional arrangements they experience in today's schools.

We use metaphors whenever we attempt to understand one entity or experience in terms of another. Thus, in these teacher-written stories, metaphor proceeds through the implicit or explicit assertions that the person or experience they describe is (or is like) the image portrayed in one of the collages. It is both the strength and the weakness of metaphor that in highlighting certain interpretations, metaphor tends to force other conceptions into a background role. In their storied tellings, much as with the collages, the metaphors for women's identities were presented in the grotesque—each vignette concentrates on features that persuade the reader to see in their examples the effects of particular social institutions and practices. It is the purpose of critical stories to move beyond theory and method to empower teachers and other storytellers to see for themselves power structures, social myths and, in this case, stereotypes of gender roles, as they are played out and institutionalized in the public space of schools. The stories teachers told tended to be *artful;* they were very descriptive—packed with colorful language—and they were boldly opinionated, politically charged, and alive with emotion.

What stories were teachers compelled to tell? Upon sharing the twelve metaphors with three groups of master's level teachers, 66 teachers provided life-history, anecdotal, essay responses to the metaphors they were given. Seven male teachers responded.[2] The numbers of essays were as follows: Gaea (16), dominatrix (3), good girl (1), princess (1), daughter (5), amazon queen (3), lady liberty (5), Joan of Arc (3), barbie (1), vamp (1), queen (2), and warden (25).

Mother and warden images were the most common descriptors for teachers' identity stories. The warden stories held the most surprises for me. Overwhelmingly, writers who described themselves or former teachers as wardens cast the warden as being a positive role. Only two writers stated explicitly that they wished they did not have to play the role of the warden; two were ambiguous about the role, but found it to be a necessary function of teaching, given the discipline problems in their classrooms. The other 21 wardens expressed their admiration for successful teacher-wardens and argued that wardens run strict, organized, and highly productive classrooms.

In contrast to wardens, earth mothers were described as caring and warm. In several instances these writers opined that the need to provide nurturing care, comfortable and inviting classroom environments, and values instruction superseded their interest in subject–matter-specific teaching. Like the wardens, these teachers found nurturing to be a necessary function of teaching, and cited the specific-needs children in their care. Two women who chose the Gaea image were pregnant at the time of the writing. Both are elementary school teachers. One of these teachers expressed her surprise and discomfort that more than one of the parents had asked her how she would explain her pregnancy to the children. "I'm married," she said, "and I'm intimate with my husband. Should I pretend that this was an immaculate conception? Clearly, the parents who asked were uncomfortable with my being a sexually active woman, even if my partner was my marriage partner."

Probably because there was a lack of clear distinctions between the categories, the good girl, princess, daughter, and Barbie images overlapped in the teacher-contributed essays. Powerlessness is the overweening commonality among the images. For instance, the images of princess and girl encompassed the notion of purity—delicacy, cleanliness, and a person who is physically unimposing in either her sexuality or her physical strength. Taken together, there were eight essays that offered the vulnerable girl image, all written by female teachers. In all but one of these, the "girl" role was defined in positive terms. The one exception was a self-reflective piece in which the writer describes herself as a "good girl" in the first few years of her teaching experience, telling a story about a particular parent interaction in which she relied on girlishness to get her through an uncomfortable relationship. This teacher goes on to comment, however, that through the trials of experience, she finds herself emerging into a stronger person who will eventually have the confidence to assume leadership roles.

Similar to the girlish persona, the amazon queen, lady liberty, Joan of Arc, and queen images can be thought of as a single category (totaling 13 responses). The common features in these metaphors are personal strength and maturity, but only the lady liberty descriptor speaks directly to maternal qualities. The lady liberty image recalled very positive experiences of schooling for the writers. Most remembered someone from their own educational history, but two described current colleagues. The amazon queen images were tonally less positive—and two of the three were written about African American colleagues (with one Gaea image about an African American woman, there were a total of four essays that described African American educators). Within the structure of these two metaphors, lady liberty and the amazon queen, teachers found openings to present descriptions of colleagues whose sexuality they questioned. Although the word "lesbian" never crossed the page of any of the writers, hints and innuendoes abounded.

The dominatrix and the vamp were the only metaphors that drew remembrances of sexually explicit behaviors by teachers. The two dominatrix stories contributed by male teachers describe instances in which they believed their (female) teachers had flirted with students and flaunted their bodies in ways that made them uncomfortable with their own early, developing sexual identities when they were students. The two women who drew from these metaphors portrayed colleagues who used their sexuality to attain favors from male administrators in the workplace.

Critical Discourse

In the third inquiry phase of this project, we—teacher/participants—began to explore the implications of our metaphors and stories for understanding the roles of women in schools, and we began to assess the possible implications these images might hold for constructions of women's identity in society more generally.[3] For my own part, I was particularly interested to understand how teachers had come to believe that "teacher as warden" holds positive implications for schooling, and I wanted to explore with teachers the possible negative connotations of mothering images for teachers. Our conversations took in the implications of standards-driven curricula for creating an environment in which control and order are equated with efficient production standards. We also discussed varying conceptions of the purpose of education. We talked about fear. We contemplated, together, what schools and teaching look like when we suppose their main purpose to be the preparation of students to be better workers, especially as we struggled to understand the impact of preparing the workforce under the watch-dog scrutiny of businessmen and politicians who decry the failure of schools (and the mostly female teaching corps; see Grumet, 1993).

Further, we considered the possibility that, as teachers, we must engage in some forms of "armed love," as Paulo Freire (1998) teaches, and that "we must dare, in the full sense of the word, to speak of love without the fear of being called ridiculous, mawkish, or unscientific, if not antiscientific" (pp. 340–341). Yet, our lovingness need not make us coddlers of undisciplined little delinquents (p. 15); rather, we can engage in loving teacher/student relationships without abandoning discipline in the classroom and respect for other students, teachers, and learning. Further, we explored the possibility that "mothering" as a teaching metaphor is inconsistent with maintaining mutual respect for the different roles of teachers and parents, and we explored the possible patriarchal implications for women who accept the role of mothers who teach (e.g., the politics of hierarchy, authority, and economics).

Throughout these critical dialogues with teachers, I have done my best not to contradict my words with my deeds. It would be so much easier to claim on the authority of the role of the professor the correctness of my beliefs than it is to accept that many, if not most, teachers in my classes will never acknowledge that "We are political militants because we are teachers" (Freire, 1998, p. 58). By speaking about these matters in a climate of mutual respect and tolerance, however, I believe we achieved something that is sometimes unique in educational settings; that is, we shared an educational space that allowed the free exploration and sharing of ideas, despite differences of opinion that disposed us to criticize, question, and debate in our expressions of our disagreement.

The purpose of critical discourse is to bring about an iterative learning experience in which knowledge is shared and developed through a conversational exchange of ideas. Although participants in the discourse occupy different spaces (e.g., author/presenter and reader/participant) they share a pedagogic project of exploring and sharing what each knows in a mutually informative teaching moment. In consequence of critical dialogue, theoretically, reflective teacher-learners then engage in renewed contemplation of their place as an actor in the world, considering the social, political, economic, and cultural contexts of teaching, knowing, and learning.

Back to the Drawing Board

To continue the cycle of symbolic (re)presentation, critical storytelling, critical discourse, and symbolic (re)formation, I entered the fourth (but not final) inquiry phase of this project. In this phase, I have (re)presented (re)assessed and (re)created women's identity metaphors in a multimedia, collaged, visual text captured on the CD, *Dancing the Data Too*.[4] My collaged representations have been combined with written words, sound tracks, and musical improvisations. I include teachers' stories, teachers' experiences, and snippets of the social and political discourse that arose during the critical dialogue phase of the inquiry. The willful combination of images in this media "bath" advances a vision of the future made up of fragments of the present and past. Drawing from the rich array of teachers' stories obtained from the inquiry, I again used collage as a mode through which to (re)interpret both the stories teachers told and their underlying social myths.

In creating and arranging these images, I found myself negotiating dangerous territory. It is important to me that this work should not contribute to pervasive negative and harmful representations of women and, paradoxically, that it should in some way freeze in place the iconic images through which both men and women frame their ideas about what it means to be a woman. The possibility that my images would reify the stereotypes that they were intended to portray introduced a sort of tension to the work. To counteract that possibility, it became necessary to emphasize discordant images—and to encourage the notion that image was being "played" with in mischievous ways. I tried to introduce noise to the visual text of the collage, not for the simple pleasure of chaos, but because I had chosen to use the everyday reality of multiplicity and heterogeneity of ideas about the roles of women and teachers as images to encourage provocateurs to renew (my own and my viewers') efforts to envision social norms as if they could be otherwise.

This cycle of (re)presentation/(re)interpretation will continue if the multimedia collages that are included in the compact disk inspire dialogue and discourse among readers and viewers as I intend. From reactions, stories, and reinterpretations of these layered embodiments of women's ways of being, I (and others) can interpret and reinterpret embodied women's myths in a larger project to rewrite women's roles in society and transform existing gendered inequalities. The compact disk collage is only one representation of my interpretations of this inquiry. For me, the most important rendering will manifest itself in my curricular choices for the teacher education courses that I teach. In my own contemplative response to this project, I have renewed my focus on my choice of reading materials, for instance, in the hope that in my role as a teacher educator I can use my courses to encourage further consideration by teachers of the possibilities for teachers and schools to (re)shape metanarratives about class, race, gender, age, and sexual orientation.

Arts-Based Approaches to Critical Pedagogy

My overarching purpose in this study was to understand how capitalistic materialism inscribes meaning in the flesh—and the clothing, and the actions and the rituals of teachers' practices—in the processes of creating, reproducing, and reifying gender definitions and stereotypes. I have attempted to investigate how social metaphors become inscribed in both the person and the role of "teacher." It was an assumption on my part that teachers are important socializing influences in the lives of children and that the ritualistic, gendered behaviors of teachers will reinforce and reproduce meanings and forms of social control that manifest themselves in hierarchical socioeconomic structures and power distributions. The fact that popular culture sweeps people into its currents yields the possibility that we might stumble under its force and, in trying to retain our balance, we might grab for support from the familiar; thus, we might remain unaware and unprobing of the deeper meanings of the events that caused us to stumble in the first place. It is my hope that this project presented opportunities for teachers to alter the currents and find new support in the unfamiliar.

In this chapter and in other writing about this inquiry, I present linear arguments that are reflective of my training in the work of social science research—shaped by the forces that have marginalized and trivialized artwork through our twentieth-century scientific value system. In contrast, my collage representations are formed in my search for imagery in the intuitive parts of my psyche. I believe that we are seeing arts-based approaches emerge on the edges of qualitative inquiry primarily because rational, pseudo-science approaches do not work in attempts to understand social phenomena that lie outside conscious rational thought. It would be a mistake to conceive of arts-based inquiry works as alternative research reports that are entertaining or interesting diversions from the typical forms of data display. Instead, arts-based research offers an alternative means for creating inquiries compatible with a critical pedagogy project that nurtures rather than alienates the individual internally and in her/his connections with the larger society. When we view the pedagogical purpose for arts-based inquiry it offers us the hope of an interpretive research model that connects humankind through its social and spiritual relevance.

Notes

1. In his 1992 discussion of critical storytelling Thomas Barone defines the phases engaged in critical storytelling and expresses the need for "an ultimate theme or central set of insights around which the emerging story can be woven" (p. 144). A trace of Barone' s discussion can be found in the structure of this inquiry effort.

2. Seven male teachers described their former teachers, whereas women had the opportunity to be self-reflective. Three men wrote about teachers who recalled mother images, one described an elementary school dominatrix, and one wrote about a high school dominatrix; another praised an elementary school warden who had been his supervising teacher during his student teaching/internship experience, and one described his experience as a "Joan of Arc" colleague.

3. Although critical discourse was an important feature of the inquiry with each of the three groups of teachers participants, the practice of critical discourse had its greatest impact on the third group of teachers. This group benefited, I believe, from

sharing information about the numbers of teachers who responded to each metaphor, as well as from a deeper revelation by me of the analysis I had made of the stories, including my opinion that both the mother and the warden images are nonbeneficial to teachers and schooling practices.

4. The original musical score is contributed by Jay Cravath, with Susan Finley.

References

Barone, T. E. (1992). Beyond theory and method: A case of critical storytelling. *Theory Into Practice, 31*(2), 142–146.

Bordo, S. (1997). The body and the reproduction of femininity. In K. Conboy, N. Median, & S. Stanbury (Eds.), *Writing on the body* (pp. 90–110). New York: Columbia University Press. (Reprinted from S. Bordo, *Unbearable weight: Feminism, western culture, and the body,* 1993, Berkeley: University of California Press)

Denzin, N. K. (1991). *Images of postmodern society: Social theory and contempora cinema.* Thousand Oaks, CA: Sage.

Finley, S. (2001). Painting life histories. *Journal of Curriculum Theorizing,* 7(3), 13–26.

Freire, P. (1998). *Teachers as cultural workers: Letters to those who dare teach.* (D. Macedo, D. Koike, & A. Oliveira, Trans.). Boulder, CO: Westview.

Grumet, M. (1993). The play of meanings in the art of teaching. *Theory Into Practice,* 32(4), 204–209.

McLaren, P. (1999). *Schooling as a ritual performance.* (3rd ed.). New York: Rowman and Littlefield.

Wittig, M. (1997). One is not born a woman. In K. Conboy, N. Median, & S. Stanbury (Eds.), *Writing on the body* (pp. 309–317). New York: Columbia University Press. (Reprinted from from M. Wittig, *The straight mind,* 1992, New York: Beacon Press)

CHAPTER 12

Frameworks of Blood and Bone: An Alchemy of Performative Mapping

TOBY DASPIT AND MORNA MCDERMOTT

Make a map, not a tracing. . . . What distinguishes the map is that it is entirely oriented toward an experimentation in contact with the real.

—Deleuze & Guattari, *A Thousand Plateaus*

Kalamazoo, Michigan (February 2001)

Memory and temporal structure are the new spaces of art to me.

—Paul Miller, *Flow My Blood*

We deliberately wait until "final" revisions to open the boxes. The two flimsy, blue, green and white boxes are stored in a musty locker on the ground floor of the apartment building where we live. Now they sit on the floor of our makeshift office (the second bedroom). The boxes don't contain everything we prepared for the 1999 *Journal of Curriculum Theorizing* (JCT) conference presentation that we focus on in this chapter—some pieces hang on our office walls; the sculptures are in our bedroom; the hat box seems to randomly pop up in various places around the apartment—but they certainly symbolize and, in our minds, re-present our efforts.

We re-member what we did in that presentation many times in compiling this chapter. And every time we re-member, every time we "perform" the act of re-collection, we are reminded of the complexity of such an endeavor. We re-member Jorge Luis Borges:

> I think that if I recall something, for example, if today I look back on this morning, then I get an image of what I saw this morning. But if tonight, I'm thinking back on this morning, then what I'm really recalling is not the first image, but the first image in memory. So that very time I recall something, I'm not recalling it really, I'm recalling the last time I recalled it. I'm recalling my last memory of it. So that really, I have no memories whatever. (qtd. in Kehl, 1983, p. 1)

But we went ahead and opened the boxes anyway. Here's what came tumbling out.

Baton Rouge, Louisiana (April, 2000)

> *[P]erformance is becoming significant because I see it as a way of translating theoretical work . .*
>
> —Petra Munro, qtd. in Marshall, Sears, & Schubert, *Turning Points*

The idea for performative mapping emerges, as most of our ideas do, out of dialogue—this time with Wanda Hurren (2000) during the First Internationalization of Curriculum Studies Conference. We are paired to present our work (Daspit & McDermott, 2000), which is essentially a distillation of our JCT presentation (we can't transport the artwork so we come with only a packet of collage images/text), with Wanda during a "conversation." Through e-mail contact, we agree to meet before the presentation to talk about performance possibilities. We know that we don't want to hear each other read "academic" papers. Prior to our presentation, we sit on stone benches outside the Student Union and discuss how we should re-present our works in dialogic fashion. We struggle over issues regarding "form" and "voice." How should we re-present our work in such a way that our individual work can be "seen" while we maintain a fluid and integrated structure? Should we?

It occurs to us that one of the most interesting prospects in our collaborative effort is not the "presenting" of *our* "individual" work, but rather the meanings created through juxtapositions inspired by each moment as pieces from Wanda's work are threaded together with our own. Furthermore, we wonder how to translate much of our work, which is visual, into something that can be read. Wanda suggests that we somehow perform what was visual in the form of verbal dialogue—an aural collage—disparate, previously "isolated" pieces recombined within the lived moment of our conversation.

Following that conversation, we continuously return to her words, tumbling the visual, aural, and spatial ideas in our heads, turning concepts over, inverting frameworks: how to hear spaces; how to see sounds? A question emerges and begins to gnaw at the periphery of our brains: How can performance and re-presentation be hybridized across the context of time and space? The question reminds us of Baudelaire's (1857/1989) "Correspondences," in which he envisions "[a]ll scents and sounds and colors meet[ing] as one" (p. 12).

Of course performances *are* inherently re-presentational, and re-presentations are always performances. But the in-between "space" of performance and re-presentation creates an experiential, aesthetic heuristic we call "performative mapping." Performative maps are means to "think," as Jacques Daignault contends, and "articulate the spaces between words and concepts" (qtd. in Pinar, Reynolds, Slattery, & Taubman, 1995, p. 482). They signify the dynamic "excluded third" (p. 483) between actions and re-presentations. They *are* living collages—reflections of/on the past, constructions of/in the present, and visions of/toward the future.

Daignault sees such "thinking the middle" as "a lightning flash, a performance that will be 'staged' " (Pinar et al., 1995, p. 482)—for us, of course, following Deleuze and Guattari (1987), the performative will be mapped. Daignault's conception of curriculum epitomizes our views of mapping the data that are our work/life/love: "By phrasing curriculum as thinking Daignault implies . . . [that] curriculum as thinking is always moving, diversifying, or to use Deleuzian terms, is 'nomadic'. . . . Curriculum does not exist, it happens" (Pinar, et al., p. 483). We follow Daignault, and hope that our work also "portray[s] thought thinking itself" (p. 485).

We map our experiences—moving landscapes traced with aesthetic and sensory hues, ruptures of memory, and overlays of imagination. Such experiences in part determine the forms re-presentative maps will take. The presentation becomes us (artist/audience) as we exist in relationship to texts, not in texts themselves. The "original" form and content of re-presentations do not remain static, but flow outward, and implode inward, at each moment they are performed, or thought. Data, possible interpretations, and re-presentational forms are transformed by multiple, emergent contexts.

Essentially, performative mapping charts geographically envisioned "lived moments" (Dewey, 1934) within a spatial and temporal framework. Such artistic re-presentations are interpretations of situated knowledges and experiences. Re-presentation becomes a fluid frame of "multilayered research possibilities that explore visual and linguistic experimentation long-repressed in the analytic economies of Western educational thought" (Jipson & Paley, 1997, p. 10). Maps, in this context, represent a "textual staging of knowledge," as Lather (qtd. in Jipson & Paley, 1997, p. 4) defines it, through the use of various forms and media, which are fluid, both spatially and conceptually. The location of any lived experience shapes, and is influenced by, the intersections, seams, and ruptures occurring through multiple dialogues between individuals, between space and objects, between thought and possibility, between memory and imagination. The re-presentation of that experience is "fixed" only for a moment. In these moments, "events find their meaning in subjective encounters where knowledge is constructed and reconstructed in every new situation. In this sense, a work of art truly exists only in the encounter" (Slattery, 1999, p. 208).

Now, sitting here, typing these words, we retrace our mental steps yet again. It occurs to us that what we accomplish in our conversation with Wanda is a work of art in itself. Using shards of memory and aesthetic residue as materials, we create a "piece" which serves not merely as a signifier to something "original" (e.g., pre-conversational presentations), but which re-present possible meanings which can only be revealed or constructed through a series of "lived" performances. We find ourselves juxtaposing multiple times and places in relationship to each other—and this again mutates into new forms, shapes, and meanings. As Appelbaum (2000) reminds us, we are always "performed by the space"—the "crucial question," he notes, "is how the space is related to as an object, and what is done with and through the space" (p. 35).

Performative mapping "stages" such moments, but always gestures toward open spaces rather than seeking conclusions to be summarized for an audience (real or imagined). Performative mapping is not linear—it does not plot two-dimensional images like traditional maps. Instead, as in a hall of mirrors, "original" images are recast and hybridized many times, and in seemingly infinite ways, with no preset frame or pattern directing where the content might reveal itself, or what might be revealed.

Gestures of re-presentation are not end products but rather catalysts in the dialogic experience between "self" and each lived moment. The product is the process, the thinking. We consider performative mapping to be analogous to alchemical transformations. Alchemy, Jung (1944/1968) argues, is ultimately a transformation of the alchemist herself through the process of sublimation and the distillation of external materials. Just as McNiff (1992) notes that the artist becomes the artwork, so too the alchemist becomes the philosopher's stone. Jung writes that "[t]he basis of the *opus*, the *prima materia*, is one of the most famous secrets of alchemy. This is hardly a surprise since it represents the unknown substance . . . [which] emanates from the individual and is consequently different in each case" (p. 317, italics in original). In performative mapping, the *prima materia* is the ongoing relationship between experience and re–presentation—new sites (of space, time, and being) to be mapped.

Here, the map unfolds from Kalamazoo to Baton Rouge to Dayton, from graduate seminars to e-mails (presented on the CD-ROM that accompanies this book), from our births to our love. We "play" with multiple ways in which performative mapping becomes "visible," where we begin to conceptualize fluid knowledge. We attempt to rupture traditional linear readings in favor of a rhizomatic approach to thinking and being. In this fluid framework, alternate possibilities and meanings can emerge.

Dayton, Ohio (October 1999)

Maps . . . relate directly to performance, to interaction.
—George Landow, *Hypertext 2.0*

Our multimedia "(auto)ethnographic 'diarama'" (Gómez-Peña, qtd. in Gómez-Peña & Sinfuentes, 1997, p. 14), is presented as an "interactive exhibit" in the basement room assigned to us at the Bergamo Center, a religious retreat. We simultaneously display the items described below in attempts to enter the "hybrid domain of performance/ installation" (Gómez-Peña & Sifuentes, n.d., n.p.), to "play . . . with ideas of 'historical time and activity'" (Wojnarowicz, 1990, p. 118). The collage process informs the entire performance/ installation. We want to replace the traditional linearity of conference presentations with multi-sensory synchronicity. "Each situation," as Greil Marcus (1989) writes, "[is] an 'ambient milieu' for a 'game of events'; each change[s] its setting, and allow[s] itself to be changed by it" (p. 164).

We begin our presentation by "setting up" the space so as to encourage our participants to interact with each piece, to become an integral part of the exhibit itself. The items we bring with us (detailed below), in the form of collage, video, music, sculpture, and written text, are altered by their re-location within this space and by the interactive presence of others. Should the video be placed in the corner? Should the collages be laid out in sequence or scattered sporadically around the room? We attempt to arrange the room as far as possible to encourage movement throughout the space, allowing for infinite combinations of "going through" each piece. There is no set sequence or order to reading the installation text. We decide to let it speak for itself rather than to provide preset interpretations of our own.

We provide a table where participants create their own collages from scraps we have gathered and used in our own collage work. Each "scrap" has emotional, geographical, and/or temporal significance to us, as the scraps were gathered during our "trips" to personally significant places at significant times in our own shared lives. We wonder what will happen when these same materials are transformed by the hands and visions of others (some of their work is presented on the CD). These pieces are shared with the group and are incorporated into a discussion about how our artwork demonstrates the elaborate interweaving between our love and work lives, about how passion informs theory and theory shapes intimate interchanges. The pieces "show" our yet unnamed theory of performative mapping—our work transformed by, and infusing, the works and ideas of others.

The next morning, in the Bergamo chapel, we talk about three "R"s that we think are essential to post-reconceptualist curriculum theorizing: recombination, re-presentation, and revelation (in Weaver, Daspit, McDermott, Ferneding, & Anijar, 1999). But, the previous morning, rather than talking *about* (Ellis, 1997), we *do*. At least we hope we do:

Collages—on plywood boards, storage box covers, picture frames, a hat box, and in a 28-page packet available for the "audience" various media, but with a common core culled from e-mail exchanges about curriculum, creativity, and love. Morna begins the collages for a class assignment at University of Virginia. Toby sits on the hardwood floor of a tiny bedroom Morna rents on his first visit to Charlottesville and helps her cut and paste, creating his first visual works since childhood, which form the heart of the packet. That summer Toby finds old e-mails on his laptop, and creates more pieces and mails them to Morna, who reassembles them as collages on plywood boards she finds near a dumpster . . . while waiting for Morna to arrive to prepare for Bergamo, Toby uses old storage box covers to continue the collaging . . . Morna arrives with collages that deliberately play with the notion of "framing" and its possibilities/limitations (e.g., a hat box) . . . she joins in constructing new box top collages.

"Audience" collages—we invite those who attend our session . . . many friends, or soon to become friends . . . to create their own collages, postcards, drawings, and so forth with materials we throw onto a table in the corner. . . . The goal is for these pieces to become part of the next installation/performance.

Video—compiled from silent home movies . . . Morna's sister Megan's seventh birthday party in Pelham, New York . . . Morna already displaying (just ask her mom) at the age of four her intense, creative personality . . . Toby's family home movies smuggled from Louisiana on 16 mm film . . . transferred in Charlottesville to video . . . the movies stop three years before he's born, but reanimate the brother he lost nearly twenty years ago . . . excerpts are cut and pasted, juxtaposing Morna and her family with Toby's family . . . "creas[ing] and tear[ing]" the "handkerchief" of time, as Michel Serres would say (qtd. Egéa–Kuehne, 1998, p. 10) . . . we call the tape "McDerpitt/Dasdermott" . . . and though it's only an 11-minute compilation, we copy it over and over so that it will loop for over two hours.

Slide show—we take our cameras on the road in the summer of 1999, attempting to meticulously document our lives . . . we travel from Kalamazoo to Long Beach Island, New Jersey (where Morna spent many childhood and adolescent summers) . . . up to New York City (Morna grew up in Pelham, a suburb outside the Big Apple), stopping in Asbury Park (Bruce Springsteen's stomping grounds) . . . and later that summer we drive to visit her mom in Hilton Head, South Carolina (where her father died), and move on to the swamps and bayous of Louisiana (where Toby was born and lived for the first

32 years of his life . . . where his brother is buried) . . . using cameras given to us by our departed family members (Morna's father's professional Nikon, Toby's brother Tommy's starter 110 Vivitar) . . . and ones acquired by us as adults (Toby's Nikon and Morna's Vivitar) . . . many of the photos emerge on collages . . . but we also display many as a slide show . . . the night before we present, we sit on the bed of the cheap motel room we rent and view the slides for the first time . . . several, through a developers' error, are double exposed . . . images originally separate fuse in startling ways . . . New Jersey/New York becomes Louisiana.

Bootleg CD—all the while, a copy of *War and Roses*, a bootleg compilation of "outtakes" from Springsteen's *Born to Run* sessions that Toby found in Charlottesville, plays softly in the background . . . Morna, having spent so much time in Jersey, Springsteen's home state . . . Toby always wanting to go there, Springsteen his confessed "savior" in high school . . . when we entered the state that summer Bruce was looping on the car stereo.

Found object sculptures—"from junk to art" (Vergine, 1997) . . . Toby cleans his car out after the summer of 1999 . . . on masonite he sculpts his documentation/interpretation of that summer with trash remaining in the car . . . Morna finds a rocking chair arm in a dumpster in Charlottesville . . . she casts her foot in plaster of Paris . . . and with sea glass and wire she creates a collage sculpture . . . one line of text excised from a magazine emerges . . . "A promise that some feelings just can't be expressed with words."

Coyote Traverses Boundaries from New York to Louisiana

Yonkers[1]

> *[O]ld stories fall apart so that new ones may form from the fragments. . . . The high gods set guard dogs around their sacred meadows. If there is to be change, its agent will have to hypnotize those dogs and slip in from the shadows, like an embarrassing impulse, a cunning pathogen, a love affair, a shameless thief taking a chance.*
>
> —Lewis Hyde, *Trickster Makes This World*

So where did we begin? I visualize Coyote snuffling under the door—whining, pacing, and scratching to get out, and when I open the door there you stand. I think of Coyote, the trickster, crossing our path and bringing with her "chance," which of course could be read as chaos, accident, or perhaps fate? And so it seems most appropriate to re-represent our lives, our experiences, and our "theor[ies] for dying . . . [and] theor[ies] for living" (Daspit, 1999, p. 77) in the form of collage—where accident is sublime, and where the unknown taunts me down the path with breadcrumbs that resemble your eyes. And I follow: "Wandering aimlessly trickster regularly bumps into things he [sic] did not expect" (Hyde, 1998, p. 95). And we create—out of fragments of memories, shards of pain, and threads of shared visions.

Coyote, the mercurial beast, symbolizes our work. Coyote, the ultimate trickster, turns things upside down, digs from the scrap heaps of our lives, and brings forward "new" items from piles of discarded leftovers (Hyde, 1998). Creating from trash is like scraping dark shadows from marrow. And in our work, in our life, we feed and are fed by these exchanges. Hence, the vampire motif in our collages. The "collage" of being a vampire?

From the beginning we "see" words as images and images as words. In our blood exchanges, we co-construct the works presented at Bergamo. Where did it start? I refuse to locate a site for beginning—we have always been in the process of "becoming," and so the past is where we start as we journey toward perpetual emergence—the snake shedding its skin. But, if I *must* pinpoint "origin" on the map of my soul, it begins with our e-mail exchanges. Words, phrases, poems, quotes—all removed from their e-mail contexts and pasted onto various locales—box tops, hat boxes, plywood, journal pages. Anywhere we can, we post our words into aesthetic recombinations to paint new visions. I draw images in response to your words. You paint words in response to my visual texts. A dialogue between self and other, image and word, desire and vision. Our work was/is who we were/are. Sometimes scraps are gathered from random sites—flyers, magazines, and store receipts become part of the arrangement. Things that had been just lying around, unnoticed, bereft of meaning. Like my life before you. From rubbish piles our collaged life emerges—"dirt-work" (Hyde, 1998, p. 182).

Lafayette[2]

> *[T]he point of curriculum study can be conceived of as a search for vision, for revelation that is original, unique, and that opens*

> *the knowing and appreciative eye to worlds hitherto unseen and unknown.*
>
> —William F. Pinar, *"The White Cockatoo"*

So where did we begin? You ask me who I am, how I define myself creatively.[3] And I say:

> I am a poet hungry (actually starving I think I said) for poetry/trying to arch and bend the tongue of language . . . to articulate the ineffable/. . . "sweet madness"/slitting the veins open and "bleeding" through/onto some medium—"aesthetic bliss"/re-combine, re-assemble, re-organize, accept, confront, and challenge chaos/delicious craft of arranging and rearranging words/it is the art/act of living, loving, of lollipop dreams, simplistic minimalism from the "bones"/is really gut wrenching insight/tough and tender . . . bone shattering/teeth scraping against curved necks/inspiration . . . perspiration . . ./The realization that I'll never see my brother alive again/I want to live the way I create. (Daspit & McDermott, 2000, n.p.)[4]

I try, from some unidentifiable moment in my doctoral studies, to find a "language" that would approach Pinar's (my major professor's) "vision" for curriculum work. I try to accept the "challenge" that Bill Pinar proposes—"the challenge . . . to attempt . . . writing that aspires to, and at times exemplifies, the revelatory function of art. Such scholarship . . . takes flight, widens the eye, and reveals anew the world which comes to form through our imagination, our labor, indeed, our lives" (p. 249).

I *think* of curriculum as collage, as poetry. I *quote* the "right" people (e.g., Block, 1998, who beautifully extends the metaphor of collage to curriculum). But I am trapped in the metaphoric. I can't run my fingers through the muddy clay of *doing*, of *being*. Then you lock eyes with me and my fingers, conduits to written language, are no longer enough.

You bring me a collage of snow and blood and sweat and sleep, spill open the colors of language without words, music without sound. You translate my Rimbaudian (1976) impulses—after all, I am envious of the way he turned vowels into colors (p. 123) and "made the whirling world stand still" (p. 115). While trying to tell you that I love you without saying the words (remember, in the days before our skin touched?), I send you Nick and Jan's (Paley & Jipson, 1997) article that I stumble across in the library. Hiding (but not too carefully I hope) in the jangled, alternatively formatted text, is the "simple" answer/question of what draws two people together into a collaborative life: "Is it love?" (p. 61). And thus ensues the collapse of logos and eros, public and private. Thus begins our love/life.

And then I paint. I sketch. I sculpt. I photograph. I montage videos. I dance. Yes, I *dance*. In us, I finally taste what I was hungry for throughout my graduate program, throughout my life. New tongues to translate the noise. As simple as collage. As intricate as relations, as living/loving.

Yes, There Really Is a Kalamazoo[5]

> I am thinking that the more I write, the more convinced I am that writing . . . is time. Is change, rhythm. Those movements of time. . . . If writing is time, as I suspect, what would writing look like outside of linear narrative or time? . . . The need for narrative and the simultaneous need to escape the prison–house of the store . . . What is the essay in this situation?
>
> —Kathy Acker, *Bodies of Work*

Wanda Pillow (2000) declares that "[p]erhaps what we need more of . . . are examples of what postmodern research looks like, does, and is committed to . . . more working examples of what it may be" (p. 23). This is a guiding force in the writing of this chapter and in our other work—performances/installations, collages, pedagogy, loving—performative maps all. And while there are obvious constraints, limits, and expectations, we deliberately play with the very notion of writing such an essay, echoing Acker's wonderment at what such an endeavor *is*.

While we agree with Peterson's (1998) assertion that in "recognizing our multiple selves and learning to integrate them, we must sometimes reinvent our methods . . . [and] reinvent our texts" (p. 8), we do wonder about the "value" of our ruminations, our collaboration, even our exhibitions of love. We concur with Paley and Jipson (2000), who note:

> [W]e find ourselves still struggling with basic questions of what collaboration really means and how it does and does not take place. We wonder about its relation to our individual and social worlds, and its value in helping us

> understand ourselves and our present environments. We puzzle, still, over how to articulate these concerns and represent the issues they have raised. (p. xii)

And while we nod our heads at poet Regie Gibson (n.d.) when he says that "this/eroticism/of/language . . . . is/more/than/the/sum/of/its/parts" (p. 1), we are concerned with what this "sum" is, as are Jipson and Paley (1997), who question the "power relations" that we perhaps unknowingly "re/produce" (p. 7) when engaging in alternative textual strategies—when we performatively map.

Nevertheless, we look backward and forward into our "present" love/work relationship. Our shared visions, our passions for each other, our memories, act as the "data" of our work. Our work embodies the rhythms of our daily lives—from the mundane (vacuuming water out of a flooded basement) to the torrid (jealous midnight screams). The professional and personal clearly overlap for us in distinct ways, blurring boundaries, where work becomes erotic and the erotic becomes . . .? What does it mean to discuss phenomenology while taking a bath? What does it mean to make us the object of study? We share the traits of Coyote, who "can encompass opposites" and who shatters the "rigid notion that everything is explicable in terms of cause and effect" (Combs & Holland, 1990, p. 101). The paradox that often when we "fight" we cannot write about our work, and yet we share the pervasive and (usually) sublime realization that without the "us" the work would not exist.

Sometimes "I" in this chapter is Morna. Sometimes Toby. Sometimes "we" is Toby. Sometimes Morna. Sometimes we speak in the third person. And so we wonder, as Roethke (1975) does, "Which I is *I*" (p. 231, italics in original), which *we* is *us*?

Notes

1. Morna's birthplace.
2. Toby's birthplace and "home" for 32 years.
3. In a course on creativity Morna took at the University of Virginia, in spring 1999, one of the requirements was to interview a "creative" person.
4. To complete the aforementioned course, Morna composed this "found" poem from fragments of responses Toby made to questions generated over e-mail. Who is the author?
5. When running an internet (Yahoo) search on the question, "Is there really a Kalamazoo?" over 8,000 "web page matches" were found. The phrase, "Yes, there really is a Kalamazoo," yielded over 2,000 "hits."

References

Acker, K. (1997). *Bodies of work: Essays.* London: Serpent's Tail.

Appelbaum, P. (2000). Performed by the space: The spatial turn. *Journal of Curriculum Theorizing, 16*(3), 35–53.

Baudelaire, C. (1989). Correspondences. (R. Wilbur, Trans.). In M. & J. Mathews (Eds.), *The flowers of evil.* New York: New Directions. (Original work published 1857)

Block. A. (1998). Curriculum as affichiste: Popular culture and identity. In W. F. Pinar (Ed.), *Curriculum: Toward new identities* (pp. 325–341). New York: Garland.

Combs, A., & Holland, M. (1990). *Synchronicity: Science, myth, and the trickster.* New York: Paragon House.

Daspit, T. (1999). "Nothing's died; it just got buried": Theory as exhumation, as duty dance. In M. Morris, M. A. Doll, & W. F. Pinar (Eds.), *How we work* (pp. 71–78). New York: Peter Lang.

Daspit, T., & McDermott, M. (2000). Untitled [On-line]. Available: http://unix.cc.wmich.edu/mmcdermo/tby1.htm

Daspit, T., & McDermott, M. (2000, April). *Post–Hybrid correspondences: Liquid frameworks and kaleidoscopic visions in alchemical curriculum theorizing.* Paper presented to the First Internationalization of Curriculum Studies Conference, Baton Rouge, LA.

Deleuze, G., & Guattari, F. (1987). *A thousand plateaus: Capitalism and schizophrenia.* (B. Massumi, Trans.). Minneapolis: University of Minnesota Press.

Dewey, J. (1934). *Art as experience.* New York: Berkley Publishing.

Egéa–Kuehne, D. (1998). Michel Serres's connections through the multiplicity of time: A metaphor for curriculum. *Journal of Curriculum Theorizing, 14*(4), 8–13.

Ellis, C. (1997). Evocative autoethnography: Writing emotionally about our lives. In W. G. Tierney & Y. S. Lincoln (Eds.), *Representation and the text: Re-framing the narrative voice* (pp. 115–139). Albany: State University of New York Press.

Gibson, R. (n.d.). *Gathering wind: The book before the book.* Chicago: Nappyhead Press.

Gómez-Peña, G., & Sifuentes, R. (1997). *Temple of confessions: Mexican beasts and living santos.* New York: Powerhouse Books.

Gómez-Peña, G., & Sifuentes, R. (2001). *"El Mexterminator I" (ethno–cyborgs and artificial savages)* [On-line]. Available: http://www.telefonica.es/fat/egomez.html

hooks, b. (1995). *Art on my mind: Visual politics.* New York: The New Press.

Hurren, W. (2000, April). *Spatial aspects of inter/national curriculum studies.* Paper presented to the First Internationalization of Curriculum Studies Conference, Baton Rouge, LA.

Hyde, L. (1998). *Trickster makes this world: Mischief, myth, and art.* New York: Farrar, Straus & Giroux.

Jipson, J., & Paley, N. (Eds.) (1997). *Daredevil research.* New York: Peter Lang.

Jung, C. G. (1968). *Psychology and alchemy.* (2nd ed.). (R. F. C. Hull, Trans.). Princeton, NJ: Princeton University Press. (Orignal work published 1944)

Kehl, R. (Ed.). (1983). *Silver departures: A collection of quotations.* La Jolla, CA: Green Tiger Press.

Landow, G. (1997). *Hypertext 2.0: The convergence of contemporary critical theory and technology.* Baltimore: The Johns Hopkins University Press.

Marcus, G. (1989). *Lipstick traces: A secret history of the twentieth century.* Cambridge, MA: Harvard University Press.

Marshall, J. D., Sears, J., & Schubert, W. H. (2000). *Turning points in curriculum: A contemporary American memoir.* Upper Saddle River, NJ: Merrill.

McDermott, M., & Daspit, T. (1999). *Opus(alchemical)contra(correspon . . .)naturam(. . . dences): Infusions, transfusions, and reve(a)lations in curriculum theorizing.* Interactive exhibit at the 21st Annual JCT Conference on Curriculum Theory and Classroom Practice, Dayton, OH.

McDermott, M., & Daspit, T. (in press). Alchemical transformations: Infusions, transfusions, and reve(a)lations in curriculum theorizing. In W. Reynolds & J. Webber (Eds.), *Curriculum dis/positions.* Mahwah, NJ: Lawrence Erlbaum.

McNiff, S. (1992). *Art as medicine.* Boston, MA: Shambala Publications.

Miller, P. (1995). Flow my blood the DJ said (excerpt). Liner notes from *Song of a dead dreamer.* New York: Asphodel.

Morris, M. (1999). Intellectual response–ability and the unconscious. *Journal of Curriculum Theorizing 15*(1), 9–12.

Paley, N., & Jipson, J. (1997). Personal history: Researching literature and curriculum (literal, alter, hyper). *English Education, 29*(1), 59–69.

Paley, N., & Jipson, J. (2000). *Questions of you and the struggle of collaborative life.* New York: Peter Lang.

Peterson, P. (1998). Why do educational research? Rethinking our roles and identities, our texts and contexts. *Educational Researcher, 27*(3), 4–10.

Pillow, W. S. (2000). Deciphering attempts to decipher postmodern educational research. *Educational Researcher, 29*(5), 21–24.

Pinar, W. (1991). "The white cockatoo": Images of abstract expressionism in curriculum theory. In G. Willis & W. Schubert (Eds.), *Reflections from the heart of educational inquiry: Understanding curriculum and teaching through the arts* (pp. 244–249). Albany: State University of New York Press.

Pinar, W., Reynolds, W., Slattery, P., & Taubman, P. (1995). *Understanding curriculum: An introduction to the study of historical and contemporary curriculum discourses.* New York: Peter Lang.

Rimbaud, A. (1976). *Arthur Rimbaud: Complete works.* (P. Schmidt, Trans.). New York: Harper & Row.

Roethke, T. (1975). *The collected poems of Theodore Roethke.* New York: Anchor Books.

Slattery, P. (1999). Popular culture and higher education: Using aesthetics and seminars to reconceptualize curriculum. In T. Daspit & J. Weaver (Eds.), *Popular culture and critical pedagogy* (pp. 201–218). New York: Garland.

Turner, G. (1999, February). Saint Sebastian. *Borderlines, 48,* 5–9.

Vergine, L. (Ed.). (1997). *Trash: From junk to art.* Milan: Electa.

Weaver, J., Daspit, T., McDermott, M., Ferneding, K., & Anijar, K. (1999, October). *Beyond reconceptualization.* Panel discussion at the 21st Annual JCT Conference on Curriculum Theory and Classroom Practice, Dayton, OH.

Wojnarowicz, D.(1990). *Tongues of flame.* New York: Distributed Art Publishers.

Contributors

LESLIE BABINSKI is an Assistant Professor in the Education Department at Bucknell University where she teaches courses in school psychology and school counseling. Her research interests include supporting beginning teachers through consultee-centered consultation and the long-term outcomes for children with ADHD. She graduated from the University of California, Berkeley, in 1993 with a doctorate in Educational and School Psychology.

CARL BAGLEY is Director of the B.A. (Hons.) degree in Childhood and the Arts in the School of Education at the University of Durham in the United Kingdom. His research interests and publications are in the field of qualitative methodology and educational policy. He is coauthor of *School Choice and Competition: Markets in the Public Interest?* (Routledge)

DONALD S. BLUMENFELD-JONES is an Associate Professor of Curriculum Studies at Arizona State University. His main research interests are the relation between the arts and educational research, critical social theory and curriculum, hermeneutics and curriculum, and the place of authority in education as a curricular issue. He was, for 20 years, a professional modern dancer. He continues to write poetry and dance on occasion.

MARY BETH CANCIENNE teaches in the Creative Arts in Learning Division at Lesley University in Cambridge, MA. Her research interests and publications are in the fields of curriculum theory, arts-based methodology, and teacher education. She explores movement and dance as a method for theorizing, researching, and teaching. She lives in Charlottesville, Virginia.

TOBY DASPIT, "Sparky," and MORNA MCDERMOTT, "Max," love/live together in Kalamazoo, Michigan, where they both teach in the College of Education at Western Michigan University. Toby is the coeditor of the forthcoming book, *Imagining the Academy: Higher Education and Popular Culture* and *Science Fiction Curriculum, Cyborg Teachers, and Youth Culture(s)* (Peter Lang). Morna recently completed her Ph.D. at the University of Virginia. Her dissertation, *"Flinging the Piano" of Critical Post Avant-Garde Inquiry: A Study of Four Pre-Service Teachers' Collaged Representations of Self and Pedagogy,* explores methods and aims of arts-informed inquiry in education. When not collaging theories of knowledge and meanings of a collaborative life (see http://unix.cc.wmich.edu/mmcdermo), they can be found watching *Buffy the Vampire Slayer* and deciding where next to travel and eat.

C. T. PATRICK DIAMOND is Professor at the Center for Teacher Development, the Ontario Institute for Studies in Education, University of Toronto, Canada. He specializes in literary forms of arts-based narrative inquiry, leadership studies, and teacher-researcher-educator development. He has led teacher institutes in Canada, Brazil, and Hong Kong and is an associate editor of *Curriculum Inquiry.* He has published some 170 works including the coauthored book, the *Postmodern Educator* (Peter Lang).

GENE DIAZ has led many lives, as an engineer, a teacher, a visual media artist, an art gallery director, and mother. She completed her Ph.D. in 1994 at the University of New Orleans and currently teaches in and directs Lesley University's Creative Arts in Learning Division, in Cambridge, MA. Her work as an educational ethnographer has focused on artists in schools, and technology in education. Although she teaches courses in curriculum theory, they always result in art-based inquiry in the form of Readers Theater.

SUSAN FINLEY teaches social and philosophical foundations and research methods at Washington State University, Vancouver. Her study was conducted in an effort to understand the reproduction of market-driven stereotypes and images of identity through informal and formal socialization in schools. Her research interests include the development and examination of arts-based approaches to educational inquiry, gender issues, and examinations that seek to develop pedagogical possibilities for educational empowerment and social justice.

PAUL FRELLICK serves as the Producing Director of the Global Arts Initiative, a program of the International Social Studies Project at the University of North Carolina at Chapel Hill, and he is the founding Artistic Director of the Deep Dish Theater Company. Previously he served as Artistic Director of Chicago's Organic Theater. His writing projects include a revue, *Politically Bent,* and a stage adaptation of Tim O'Brien's novel, *In the Lake of the Woods.*

TERRY JENOURE is a musician and educator. As the Director of the Augusta Savage Gallery at the University of Massachusetts in Amherst (UMASS) she has forged the development of a multicultural and multi-arts program, where she continues to consider the role of a gallery as a place of community access and experimentation. Terry is a Lecturer in the Department of Afro-American Studies and the School of Education at UMASS and at Lesley University's Creative Arts in Learning Program in Cambridge, MA.

J. GARY KNOWLES practices the practice of artmaking and educational inquiry so that, in his life, the two may become—one day soon—a seamless fabric of professional work. As Co-Director of the Centre for Arts-Informed Research at the University of Toronto, Canada, he encourages graduate degree candidates to take artistic and intellectual risks in their research and be counted as arts-informed scholars. His educational scholarship is located in educational journals and books as well as found hanging on walls.

JIM MIENCZAKOWSKI trained and worked in theater and the performing arts in London before moving into teaching and researching in the U.K., Australia, and the West Indies. His performance research in ethnodrama has been the subject of numerous publications in the last decade. He is currently the Dean of the Faculty of Education and Creative Arts & the Foundation Dean of the Central Queensland Conservatorium of Music at Central Queensland University (CQU), Australia.

STEVE MORGAN is a practicing psychologist in Queensland, Australia, where he was also, for many years, an academic involved in mental health nursing education. A researcher in the areas of suicide prevention and mental health education, he currently specializes in working toward the rehabilitation of the victims of serious vehicle accidents. Steve is one of the original exponents of ethnodrama performances and has published extensively with colleagues in this and other health-related areas.

CAROL A. MULLEN is Assistant Professor in the Leadership Development Department, University of South Florida, Tampa, FL. She specializes in leadership and curriculum development and uses arts-based inquiry for these purposes. She has published extensively and guest-edited nine special issues of academic journals. Her latest book is the award-winning *Breaking the Circle of One* (Peter Lang).

G. W. RASBERRY teaches in the Faculty of Education at Queen's University, Canada, where he recently completed a Postdoctoral Fellowship. He has written a number of articles in the areas of curriculum studies, writing pedagogy, and teacher education. A published poet and working musician, Gary is interested in the tangle where teacher education, aesthetic practice, and the arts come together and apart.

DWIGHT ROGERS is an Associate Professor in Elementary Education at the University of North Carolina at Chapel Hill. He is a former elementary, preschool, and kindergarten teacher and an old-time banjo player. In addition to his work with the North Carolina

Curriculum, Music, and Community Project, his research and scholarly interests include gaining a deeper understanding of the issues and concerns facing beginning teachers and the impact of student-teacher relationships on learning.

LYNN SMITH is a research associate at Central Queensland University (CQU), Australia, where she collaborates with Jim Mienczakowski on the development of theoretical constructs relating to, among other things, ethnodrama. Lynn has an extensive background in Arts Education and has lived and taught in remote communities at the "top end" of Australia. She is currently completing her master's dissertation in Arts Education at CQU.

CELESTE SNOWBER is a dancer, educator, and writer who is an Assistant Professor in the Faculty of Education with a concentration in dance education at Simon Fraser University in Burnaby, British Columbia, Canada. She has authored several books and various journal articles in connection with issues of embodiment.

SUZANNE M. THOMAS is an arts-informed researcher and a doctoral candidate at the Ontario Institute for Studies in Education at the University of Toronto, Ontario. Her current interests focus on teacher development and, together with students and teachers, she explores sense-of-place in schools and educative contexts. She is strongly committed to making educational inquiry informed by the arts accessible to a wider audience through the use of new media and public exhibit venues.

Index